UNSOLVED AVIATION MYSTERIES

FIVE STRANGE TALES OF AIR AND SEA

KEITH McCLOSKEY

First published 2020

The History Press
97 St George's Place, Cheltenham,
Gloucestershire, GL50 3QB
www.thehistorypress.co.uk

British Library Cataloguing in Publication Data.
A catalogue record for this book is available from the British Library.

ISBN 978 0 7509 9258 9

Typesetting and origination by The History Press
Printed and bound in Great Britain by TJ International Ltd.

MIX
Paper from
responsible sources
FSC® C013056

Dedicated to Norrie Simpson

CONTENTS

INTRODUCTION

This collection of five aviation mysteries all have the theme of aviation and the sea. Aircraft that disappear over the sea, lakes or rivers are always more difficult to solve or explain because in many cases they literally disappear from sight, often leaving just a tantalising clue such as a wheel, as in the case of the missing Sri Lankan Learjet or the Isle of Mull Cessna. In the case of the Mull Cessna, I believe I am publishing here for the first time three underwater photos of the wreckage of the aircraft (Cessna F.150H registered G-AVTN). The photos are part of a batch of twenty-eight slides taken in September 1986 by diver Richard Grieve, who kindly gave them to me. They have been seen by others, who say they are not conclusive enough, but I reproduce two (out of three) of the slides showing the registration, and the reader can then agree or disagree that this is the missing Cessna flown by Peter Gibbs on Christmas Eve 1975.

The Kinross Incident has attracted much attention from those interested in UFOs. The most puzzling aspect of this story is the manner in which the F-89C Scorpion disappeared after it was seen to merge with an unidentified aircraft (supposedly a Canadian military aircraft) on a radar screen. Not a single trace of it was found on the surface of Lake Superior.

The Learjet that carried Sri Lankan businessman Philip Upali Wijewardene also disappeared from radar screens as it approached the coast of Indonesia. Apart from a wheel, this too has left no other trace and the question remains as to why it suddenly disappeared as it was climbing towards a height of 39,000ft (11,887m).

Although some may say the JFK story can be explained, there are also many who feel there is more to the loss of the aircraft than first appears. There is also the other aspect of a seeming curse that hangs over the family, particularly with respect to aviation.

The last chapter concerns the case of businessman Alfred Loewenstein. The story involves the death of a man, rather than the disappearance of a plane, but nonetheless it is one of the most intriguing stories in aviation mysteries. Quite simply, he did not have the strength to open the aircraft door on his own, so how did he fall 4,000ft (1,219m) to his death in the English Channel?

I hope the reader finds these stories interesting, also bearing in mind that each one involves the tragic loss of life.

Keith McCloskey
Berkshire
June 2019

CHAPTER 1

THE ISLE OF
MULL CESSNA

The Isle of Mull is the second largest island of the Inner Hebrides after Skye. Despite its size, it has always had a fairly low population, with the small town of Tobermory acting as the main centre on the island. The island is known for tourism and its whisky, but despite being 90 miles from Glasgow, it used to require an eight-hour journey by road/rail and ferry to get there. With the advent of Scottish airline Loganair in the early 1960s, a proposal was put forward to establish an airfield on Mull. Army sappers cleared an area near Salen of 50,000 tonnes of earth and 1,000 trees to lay out a 780ft (238m) grass runway in only fifty-four days.

Once the airstrip was ready, Loganair started a service from Glasgow to Mull via North Connel, which was the airfield for Oban. The service ran at weekends in the summer and eventually became a daily service during the summer months. The schedule continued until 1975, when it was dropped as not being viable, which was a blow to the tourist economy of the island. However, the airstrip with the adjoining Glenforsa Hotel proved to be popular with private flyers, who would fly in and park their aircraft there, stay at the hotel and explore the island. The hotel had almost burned down in 1968 and was rebuilt in a Norwegian log style with chalets. In the same year that Loganair discontinued its summer service from Glasgow, the Glenforsa strip became the scene of one of the most enduring mysteries in Scotland to date.

On 20 December 1975, two guests arrived at the hotel, Norman Peter Gibbs and his companion, university lecturer Dr Felicity Grainger. They had visited previously on a few occasions and enjoyed the laid-back atmosphere of the area. Gibbs, who used Peter as his first name, was a 53-year-old property developer and had formed a company named Gibbs and Rae with a partner. He had come to Mull on holiday but also tohave a look at property in the area with a view to buying a place he could turn into a hotel with some land, where he could make an airstrip for visiting aircraft. What had given him the idea was the Glenforsa Hotel itself, with its own airstrip.

The two of them had driven to the Glenforsa Hotel by car having travelled over from Oban on the ferry. Gibbs was a pilot and had served in the RAF during the Second World War. After his arrival, he was advised that there was an aircraft for hire at North Connel airfield at Oban. The aircraft was Cessna F.150H G-AVTN and its owner was a well-known person named Ian Robertson Hamilton, a local market gardener and businessman and one of the four men who had stolen the Stone of Destiny from Westminster Abbey on Christmas Day in 1950. After a phone call from Gibbs to Hamilton, it had been intended that Hamilton was to fly the Cessna from North Connel over to Gibbs at the Glenforsa Hotel strip and Gibbs would then fly Hamilton back to North Connel before returning to Mull. It was a fairly short journey each way of around twenty minutes, and with the time taken for the formalities of handing the Cessna over to Gibbs when he arrived at Glenforsa and Gibbs landing at North Connel to drop Hamilton off and take off again the whole exchange should have taken well under two hours. However, the weather, which was to play a significant part in this story, intervened and so Hamilton rang Gibbs to say he could not fly over. From all accounts, Gibbs was never one to let anything stand in his way, so he arranged with Hamilton that he would drive over on the ferry from Mull to Oban with Grainger, meet Hamilton and return himself with the aircraft. Grainger would then drive the car back to the hotel.

Once back at the Glenforsa Hotel, both Gibbs and Grainger spent the next few days looking at property in the area and taking the time to relax.

On Christmas Eve, the two of them set off from the Glenforsa airstrip in the Cessna to the Isle of Skye and returned at 4.30 p.m. It was Gibbs' birthday the following day as well as being Christmas Day, so they had an evening meal with wine in the hotel rather than go out. At 9.30 p.m., after he had finished his meal, Gibbs made an extraordinary decision and told his companion that he wanted to take the Cessna up for a quick circuit. It was a dark night with clouds and the airstrip had no facilities for night flying. Gibbs must have had some inkling that what he was about to do entailed some risk because he assured Grainger that if he got into trouble, he would bring the wheels down into the water to slow the aircraft down, then escape and make his way to the shore.

Unknown to Gibbs was the fact that the weather was shortly going to deteriorate rapidly. Gibbs should have phoned for a forecast but chose not to. He changed and then informed Roger Howitt (one of the hotel owner's sons) that he was about to undertake a quick circuit in the Cessna. Gibbs asked Grainger to place two torches for him at the end of the runway for him to use as a guide to landing. They both walked out to the Cessna and got in. Gibbs started the engine and let it run for a while before taxiing to the end of runway 26 at the eastern end of the strip. Grainger got out of the aircraft and placed the torches on the end of the runway. She then walked to a nearby fence to wait for him to carry out the short flight. Gibbs taxied to the other end of the runway and again ran the engine for a number of minutes. He then released the brakes and gathered speed down the grass airstrip to take off.

Grainger watched as the Cessna took off and made a right turn to come back parallel to the airstrip. The plane then made another right turn to come around to line up and begin its descent for landing, when it disappeared behind a group of trees beyond the runway end. It was the last time anyone would see Peter Gibbs alive and the last time anyone would see the aircraft, which, at the time of writing, has yet to be 'officially' found and recovered.

Grainger waited for some time and when it was apparent that there was no sign of the Cessna, she made her way back to the hotel. Once it was clear that Gibbs and the Cessna had disappeared, the RAF Kinloss Mountain Rescue Team, based at Fort William, were called in immediately and police and local volunteers started searching the hills. Around forty-five searchers went out each day and were spread fairly widely as they were looking for an aircraft rather than a body on its own. These searches lasted for five days, in extremely bad weather.

Due to the holiday period at the time of the disappearance, there were no fishing boats out in the sound, so other than the witnesses at the Glenforsa Hotel, nobody else had seen what happened. The strong possibility that the Cessna may have come down into the Sound of Mull itself led to a search with Royal Navy Sea King helicopters. Unfortunately, they found nothing and the search on land and over the Sound of Mull was called off.

After the searches had been called off, life started to return to normal and the general feeling was that both the Cessna and Gibbs had gone down into the sea with the possibility that they would never be found. However, on 21 April 1976, almost exactly four months after the disappearance, Glenforsa Farm Manager and shepherd Donald McGillivray was out walking across the high ground above the Glenforsa Hotel when he came across a body lying on a tree trunk. The spot where he found the body was roughly 400ft above sea level and over a mile away from the hotel. It was the body of Peter Gibbs.

The discovery of Gibbs' body sparked another bout of intensive searching for nearly a week with, again, a similar number of people (forty-plus) involved. However, there was no sign of the Cessna and no other sign of how Gibbs might have reached the spot he was found in. The discovery of his body raised more questions than answers in what was turning into a peculiar tale.

The system for investigating deaths in Scotland is different to the rest of the UK. There is no system of coroners' inquests in Scotland as there is in England, Wales and Northern Ireland. Accidental, unexpected, unexplained, sudden or suspicious deaths are investigated privately for the local crown agent, an official called the Procurator Fiscal. Only certain types of death are investigated further at Fatal Accident Inquiries (FAIs). Gibbs' death fell into the category of requiring an FAI and this was duly held in Oban on 24 June 1976. The Board of Trade Senior Accident Inspector William Black Cairns was the first to give evidence at the inquiry. Cairns had spent eleven years in the RAF with a further eighteen years of test-flying experience behind him, totalling over 10,000 hours of flying time. He had arrived in Oban on 2 January 1976, nine days after the Cessna had disappeared and two days after the search had been called off. (At this point Gibbs was assumed to be with the missing aircraft.) Cairns gave an outline of the servicing of Cessna F.150H G-AVTN, that it was maintained by a company in Edinburgh (Lowland Aero Services) and that the certificate of registration and certificate of airworthiness were both in order. Cairns was asked if there was anything at all about the Cessna that would have suggested it had not been looked after properly or was in such a condition that it was dangerous to fly, to which he replied no.

When it came to the background of Peter Gibbs and his suitability as a pilot, a slightly different picture began to emerge. Cairns said that Gibbs was an ex-RAF pilot and after the end of the war had subsequently joined the

RAF Reserve with the rank of flying officer. Gibbs held a private pilot's licence, which Cairns said had expired in October 1974, a full year and two months before the Cessna went missing. The renewal of a licence was dependent on the pilot's age and in Gibbs' case, he was required to renew it every twelve months. The renewal of Gibbs' licence was also dependent on him passing a medical examination, which he had undertaken in May 1975. Following the medical, Gibbs applied for the licence renewal, only to be told that he would have to undergo a general flying test before it could be renewed. The records show that Gibbs did not bother to take the test for whatever reason. Flying with an out-of-date licence might be viewed as a lesser offence by some, especially as Gibbs was only flying himself in a light aircraft on the lowest category of licence, but Cairns stated that Gibbs 'was flying illegally'.

There was also a further issue with regard to the licence, because the medical undertaken by Gibbs on 10 July 1975 found that his eyesight was defective; a condition was attached to the medical certificate that stated Gibbs had to wear spectacles when he was flying. What Cairns took pains to point out was that although Gibbs had passed his medical with the condition that he would have to wear glasses whilst flying, he had not taken the general flying test, so as matters stood, his flying licence was still invalid. It is possible to argue that the invalid licence was a technicality. Gibbs had, at least, made an effort to partially renew it by taking the medical. However, the next issue raised in the inquiry was not so lightly dismissed and called into question his judgement as a competent pilot.

When Gibbs announced his decision to take the Cessna up for a quick circuit, it was already well after 9 p.m. It was also a cold, dark, cloudy night, so visibility was very poor. On top of this, snow or sleet had been forecast so the weather was set to deteriorate very shortly. Cairns was asked what experience Gibbs had of night flying and the answer was a total of only five hours. In response to the question as to whether this might be considered 'limited', Cairns replied that it was extremely limited. Despite Gibbs' lack of experience of flying at night, there was nothing to officially stop him from doing so, not-withstanding the issue over his invalid licence. The only problem that might have arisen would have been if he had taken a passenger up with him, for which he would have needed a night rating on his licence. Tied in with Gibbs' lack of experience of night flying was the problem of the Glenforsa strip itself. Cairns responded to a question as to its suitability for night-flying operations that it was not suitable at all. He went further, saying, 'As a personal opinion, with the experience I have in flying, I would certainly not attempt night flying from Glenforsa.'

At this point in the FAI, the Fiscal mentioned the very poor weather that night and then asked Cairns for his opinion as to the suitability of the two torches used by Grainger to act as landing aids. The Fiscal indicated the two torches in the room before he asked Cairns for his opinion. Cairns was scathing in his response, saying, 'In my opinion, they are absolutely worthless as a form of indication.'

The damning of the torches by Cairns was followed by his statement that the Glenforsa airstrip had no landing lights at all. Cairns then pointed out that in the absence of any wreckage of the Cessna itself, he could only make preliminary enquiries as his work was primarily concerned with an examination of the aircraft, if it was available. The Fiscal said he accepted that and put two hypothetical questions to Cairns.

The first question he asked was: Would the Cessna have been completely consumed with little or no trace if a serious fire had broken out? Cairns replied that it was unlikely as, even with a serious fire, there was always something left as wreckage. Cairns was then asked to consider if it had been possible there had been a total or partial engine failure while Gibbs was flying the plane and had made a soft landing on some part of the island. Again, Cairns responded that it was unlikely because although it was a hypothetical question, he felt that as the Cessna had been recently serviced, there was only a remote chance of that happening, unless it had run out of fuel. After prompting, Cairns did say that a stall might have been possible and that for this Cessna in landing configuration, the stalling speed would be in the region of 50mph. He made the point that if the Cessna was headed into the wind, the effective speed could have been as low as 25mph.

The Fiscal came back to the theme of the plane making a soft landing on some part of the island with the suggestion that Gibbs had jumped out and it had continued on its set course without him. Cairns didn't reject the possibility but argued that to do such a thing and open the door in a flight, which he said was most likely in a climb condition, would be a very difficult thing to do.

Furthermore, Cairns said he had never heard of anyone climbing out of a plane to jump in this way. Continuing in this argument, Cairns was asked if Gibbs would have hurt himself by jumping from a moving plane. Cairns said that he had never heard of anyone doing so and compared it to jumping from a window on the second floor of a building, and that he would expect someone jumping from a building at this height would almost certainly sustain fractures.

There followed an odd exchange between Cairns and the Fiscal. The Fiscal was presumably wanting to be clear in his mind about what exactly was involved in opening the door of a Cessna, so he asked Cairns if the pilot would step out on to the wing, to which Cairns confirmed that he would. However, the Cessna was a high-wing monoplane and a pilot opening the door would step out into nothing, other than a small footstep built into the fixed undercarriage strut. The small footstep was just an aid to getting in and out and a pilot wanting to exit could just push away from the door onto the ground or into the air as there was nothing to impede him.

The Fiscal then focused on the crux of the matter – where was the Cessna? It was Cairns' view that the plane was very unlikely to have come down in the sea surrounding Mull owing to the absence of sodium chloride in the flying boots worn by Gibbs or in his watch. These were two places where it would be expected to find evidence of salt water if someone had been in the sea. He said that the pathologist would also have expected to find traces of sea vegetation in these two places and there had been none.

On the issue of Gibbs' body being found near the top of the hill above the Glenforsa airstrip, Cairns was asked by the Fiscal to describe a situation he had been involved in concerning the loss of a light plane in the UK that had come down in a forest and had been covered over by the trees. Cairns said that the situations were different and no parallel could be drawn because the earlier accident had involved the plane coming straight down into the forest nose first and the pilot had been killed on impact. The plane had been suspended in the trees and was not found for two months.

The Fiscal was keen to examine all the scenarios as to where the Cessna may have ended up and asked Cairns if he thought the aircraft had come down in one of the hill lochs on Mull. Cairns was shown some pictures and asked if he felt that 300 yards (274m) would be enough for the Cessna to stop in if it had stalled. Cairns did not want to be drawn and replied that the pictures of the loch in question did not give any idea of dimensions or size. He did say that if it had been in a stall condition, the Cessna's undercarriage could bring it to a stop in water within a distance of 100ft (30m) and that the aircraft would eventually sink. Cairns again did not want to be drawn on whether the Cessna may have made any marks around a loch as it came down and, in fairness, it was far too generalised a question for him to give a specific answer.

Ian Robertson Hamilton, from whom Gibbs had hired G-AVTN, came into the exchange and asked Cairns to describe the radio equipment on board the Cessna that night. These were a 360 degree VHF transceiver, a VHF Omnifrequency radio finding facility, a medium-frequency radio finding facility and a radar transponder. Hamilton then produced some handling notes and asked Cairns to confirm that what was written on the back cover of the notes was a list of VHF stations along with a list of Omni-frequency stations. His aim was to show that assuming a copy was in G-AVTN, which it most likely was, then Gibbs could have chosen a station on one of the channels and be in instant communication should he have needed this. Hamilton asked Cairns to confirm that the international distress frequency was 121.5 and that no calls had been made from G-AVTN on the night of 24 December 1975. He also asked Cairns to confirm that Gibbs could have used the Omni-range unit to check his position from Omni stations at Machrihanish, the Isle of Jura, Stornoway and Prestwick. They were all listed, with their frequencies, on the back cover of the notes and Gibbs would have known how to use them. The point was that Gibbs did not try to call for help or try and check his position that night if he had been in trouble.

This led on to the area of preflight planning and whether Gibbs had carried out any. It was said of Gibbs by others later in the FAI that he was thorough in his preparation. The areas of preflight planning that Cairns expected Gibbs to have carried out included checking the following: weather condition; weather forecasting; that the radio aids were in working order; where the diversion airfield was and that it was available; the amount of fuel for the flight and that the Cessna was in a serviceable condition. Granted Gibbs was not at an airfield that had facilities but at a hotel that had little more than a grass strip. He was taking the Cessna up for one circuit and landing, which shouldn't have lasted longer than a matter of minutes from take-off to landing. In the absence of facilities at Glenforsa such as air traffic control and a meteorological office, Cairns told the FAI that he would have expected Gibbs to phone Prestwick and Machrihanish to first make sure they were available and also to get the weather forecast. At the very least, Gibbs should have dialled the local meteorological broadcast. Gibbs had done none of these things.

Going back to the invalid licence, Cairns described, in response to questions, that from the time Gibbs' licence became invalid fourteen months previously, he had flown from Biggin Hill for a total of twelve hours' flying time with an invalid licence. The line of questioning by the Fiscal seemed to suggest that Gibbs may have been getting a little 'rusty' and appeared to be trying to be fair to him by then asking if it was possible that he had been unable to use any of the VHF radio equipment due to the high ground on Mull. Cairns agreed that it was, at least, a possibility. Cairns also agreed that Gibbs would have been given everything he needed by way of notes on handling characteristics of the Cessna F.150H and would have had access to charts if he had needed them. Having set the possible scene that Gibbs had taken off with knowledge of how the Cessna handled and had got into difficulties but was unable to use the VHF equipment because of the high ground, the Fiscal asked Cairns about Gibbs making an attempt to land on the surface of a loch as the safest option. Cairns had already gone over this scenario and again repeated that it was a hypothetical situation he was not qualified to answer. When asked what he would have done in the same situation, Cairns replied that he would rather have put the Cessna down on land than water because the fixed undercarriage meant the aircraft stood a good chance of going nose first into the water as soon as it came down. Cairns did concede that the land around Glenforsa was so hilly that there would have been little option but to try and come down on water.

Cairns' examination came to an end with a question from the sheriff and Hamilton. The sheriff asked him if the landing lights would have been switched on if the Cessna was coming down to make an emergency landing and whether those lights could be seen depending on what part of the island the aircraft was coming down on. He followed this up with a final question to Cairns and that was if he (the sheriff) had been hiring an aircraft from him, whether Cairns would expect to see his licence, to which Cairns responded that he certainly would. The sheriff then asked Hamilton whether it happened that aircraft were hired from a flying club or private operator without them asking to see the pilot's licence, to which he said he had no experience of that.

Ian Robertson Hamilton was then sworn in, giving his profession as a market gardener. Before he was examined, the sheriff told Hamilton that he did not have to answer any questions that he felt might incriminate him. Hamilton confirmed he owned G-AVTN and that he had received the insurance payment in full for the £3,000 value of the Cessna. He had bought the aircraft in September 1975 and he explained that it held a General Service Certificate of Airworthiness (as opposed to a Standard Certificate of Airworthiness) which was a higher standard because it was available for hire. G-AVTN had also been extensively refurbished in March 1975 by Lowland Aero Service at Turnhouse Airport, Edinburgh, and was basically as good as new. In the time that Hamilton owned it, he said that it was maintained and kept in a good state of airworthiness. Peter Gibbs was the second person to hire the aircraft since he had bought it.

After his arrival at the Glenforsa Hotel, Gibbs had phoned Hamilton and told him that he had flown into Glenforsa before and was currently staying at the hotel and wanted to hire his Cessna. He explained that he was a qualified pilot but did not have his licence with him.

At the mention of Gibbs saying he did not have his licence with him, Hamilton said he would make a judgement as to his skills when he saw him. The original plan, he explained, was that on 21 December 1975, Hamilton was to fly G-AVTN over to the strip at the Glenforsa Hotel, meet Gibbs to confirm he could fly the aircraft and then Gibbs would fly Hamilton back to North Connel. On that day (21 December) he said the weather was below his limits for flying so Gibbs said he would drive over the following day and take the Cessna back with him. While Hamilton was explaining the plan for Gibbs to receive the aircraft, he was stopped by the Fiscal and asked to confirm that he had taken Gibbs at face value when he said that he had a flying licence and was prepared to let Gibbs take control of the aircraft without seeing the licence. Hamilton responded that he was only going to let Gibbs have the aircraft after he (Hamilton) had made some independent inquiries. The Fiscal asked him what those independent enquiries were. Hamilton replied that he had phoned the Glenforsa Hotel, who acted as airport managers for the licensee of the airstrip there, and asked them if they had information about Gibbs and whether they were satisfied he was a qualified pilot. Hamilton said that they informed him he was a qualified pilot. This appeared to be a bit of buck passing but Hamilton did say that he decided to make his mind up when he met with Gibbs and watched how he behaved in his preparation to take the Cessna back to Mull.

When asked how long Gibbs spent with the aircraft before he flew it away from Connel, Hamilton stated that Gibbs had spent half an hour going through pre-flight checks. It was a length of time, Hamilton said, that was overcautious in his view for a simple aircraft such as a Cessna F.150H. In effect, Hamilton was satisfied that Gibbs knew what he was doing, so much so that Hamilton had phoned the Glenforsa Hotel and left a message for Gibbs to call him and to arrange for him to help Hamilton brush up on some aspects of his own flying skills. It was certainly a remarkable stamp of approval from Hamilton, although he had only seen Gibbs on the ground and watched him take off for Mull.

Despite Hamilton's seal of approval, the sheriff asked him if Gibbs had mentioned using the Cessna for night flying. Hamilton said that Gibbs had not said anything about flying at night, and more to the point Hamilton felt that it was inconceivable Gibbs would have even considered using the aircraft for night flying. He said that had Gibbs asked him about it, he (Hamilton) would have refused to allow him to charter the aircraft. When he was asked why, Hamilton said that he was trying to build up flying at the North Connel airfield and felt it was important to keep well within regulations. The other reason he gave was that he considered it 'sheer folly' to attempt flying at night among mountains and near the coast, particularly in December when the weather can be particularly bad. Not only that, but when asked his opinion of Glenforsa's airstrip, Hamilton replied that he found it difficult to conceive that anyone would even attempt night flying from it. It was a strip, he said, that needed great care and concentration to get in for the first time in broad daylight, let alone even attempting night flying from it. In answer to the question did he think it foolish to attempt to fly from Glenforsa at night, he said that only by a highly experienced pilot on an ambulance flight to save a life should it be used at night.

The issue of the amount of fuel Gibbs would have had available was brought up and Hamilton estimated that Gibbs would have had enough for approximately one and a half hour's flying time from the time he took off. The only places where fuel was available on the western seaboard of Scotland, apart from his private store at North Connel, was at Prestwick, Glasgow and Stornoway.

A brief exchange followed on how often Hamilton himself used the anti-collision beacon on the Cessna, followed by Hamilton's dismissal of a number of items of wreckage that had been handed in over the previous six months as possibly being part of the wreckage. Hamilton discounted all of them, including a piece of aluminium that it was thought may have come from the Cessna.

The question that had been put to the accident investigator, Cairns, was also put to Hamilton. He was asked if it was possible that Gibbs had jumped from the Cessna while it was still in flight. He replied that it would have been almost impossible owing to the slipstream as the door was hinged from the front. Gibbs would have been seated right up against the door. This meant that at the lowest speed possible, approximately 60mph, Gibbs would have had to lean back from the door and push hard to try and open it. Leaning back from the door would have lessened the amount of pressure and leverage he could exert against it. This coupled with the fact that Gibbs would have needed to come very close to the ground, meant that he would have been unable to give close attention to flying the aircraft at such a dangerously low level and simultaneously give attention to pushing the door against the slipstream. If the aircraft had flown any slower than 60mph, Hamilton said it would have stalled. He also confirmed that Gibbs would not have been wearing a parachute as there were none on board.

When asked as to what he thought might have happened to both Gibbs and the Cessna, Hamilton explained that he had, at first, thought Gibbs may have stalled when coming in to land and come down in the sea. However, the total absence of seawater on Gibbs' clothing precluded this. He referred to the forensic report by Professor Harland of Glasgow University and said, having seen the evidence and considering there was no sign of the aircraft, along with Gibbs choosing what looked like a comfortable spot for his last rest, he felt that the aircraft had not ditched in the sea. When asked if he thought the

Cessna might have come down in a hill loch, Hamilton replied that he could not see why. Hamilton finished by stressing the pilot's notes and charts that he had made available to Gibbs contained a wealth of information. He had spent some twenty to thirty hours in the Cessna with his wife and found no reason to think it was unserviceable in any way at the time it was handed over to the care of Gibbs.

The next person to appear on the witness stand was the Chief Medical Officer for Strathclyde Police, William McLay. McLay, in company with an RAF pathologist, Squadron Leader Balfour, had carried out the post-mortem examination of Gibbs. Gibbs had been identified from his dental records and, reading from the report, perhaps the most significant item was that Gibbs had fractured the left side of the hyoid bone. The hyoid was small and located at the front of the neck, below the voice box and above the lower jaw. McLay pointed out that it must have been inflicted after Gibbs had died as there was no bruising around the area, which would be expected if Gibbs had been alive when it was broken. McLay said that it was possible that it had been caused by post-mortem decay or possibly an attack by a bird. Gibbs' neck muscles had deteriorated, but there was still sub-tissue on the bones and cartilage. This sub-tissue showed no signs of any bruising. There was little else untoward found during the post mortem and significantly, other than a small cut on his leg and the unrelated broken hyoid bone, there were no other fractured limbs, which would almost certainly be expected if Gibbs had jumped from the Cessna while it was still flying.

The other point made by McLay was that there was no sign of water in the lungs, which would have been the case if Gibbs had drowned. Neither did he inhale any seawater, which would be expected had he come down in the sea and swum to the shore. The other item of interest was what level of alcohol could be found. The organisms that produce putrefaction in the body also produce alcohol and the toxicology report found an alcohol level of 100 was found to be present. McLay was asked if it was possible that the level of alcohol in the body at the time of death would have been 'very, very much lower'. McLay agreed that it may well have been substantially lower.

Gibbs had died of exposure and McLay explained how people suffering from this are unaware that they may be dying. He said that Gibbs had probably been wandering around on a cold, wet night and may have lain down on the tree trunk to rest, whereupon he would have lapsed into unconsciousness and his body succumbed to the cold. How long Gibbs had remained conscious was a guess. People who die of exposure fall into two groups: those who lie down to rest but are not aware they are close to death and those who just lie down and basically give up. McLay also described the condition of victims taking their clothes off when they should be doing the exact opposite. This condition is known as paradoxical undressing where the victim starts to remove clothing because they feel so warm because of their blood vessels rising to the skin surface. The other thing that McLay pointed out was that there was no trace of seawater or sea vegetation and, in fact, there was nothing on the body of

Gibbs or his clothes that might have given some indication of where he had been. For instance, there were no twigs or leaves that might have shown he had made his way through a forest or thick areas of vegetation. There was nothing.

McLay was asked how long Gibbs would have been expected to survive from when he lay down at the tree. The answer was dependent on what he was wearing and his general fitness level. The clothes he was wearing were totally unsuitable for the cold, wet weather and he was not a young man and nor was he in great physical shape, even for his age. McLay gave his view that Gibbs would have lasted around six or seven hours before dying, possibly slightly more and possibly slightly less, and he would have been unconscious in the final stages. The irony of Gibbs dying where he did was that he was within a mile's walk down the hillside to the Glenforsa Hotel. McLay stated that Gibbs had virtually no injuries that would have stopped him from doing so. Neither did McLay think that alcohol had played a part in what had happened to Gibbs or affected the decisions he made.

The final conclusion of McLay's post-mortem report was that Gibbs had crash-landed the Cessna somehow, but it had been a gentle impact that had not caused him any injuries. He could not say whether the impact had been on water or land but he said it was highly unlikely that Gibbs could have jumped from the aircraft without sustaining serious injuries of some kind.

McLay was followed by an RAF dental surgeon, Flight Lieutenant Ian Hill. Flt Lt Hill was stationed at RAF Halton in Buckinghamshire and had identified Gibbs from his dental records. It was a fairly brief session and Flt Lt Hill said that his dental examination confirmed without any doubt that the body was that of Norman Peter Gibbs.

Police Constable Alexander MacLennan took the stand after Flt Lt Hill. MacLennan was stationed at Salen on the Isle of Mull. He had been phoned at 11.20 p.m. that Christmas Eve by David Howitt, part of the family who owned and ran the Glenforsa Hotel, and was told that a plane was missing. MacLennan informed officers at Tobermory and Oban. He contacted the Lochaline Hotel on the other side of the sound to see if the Cessna had landed there. When they replied they had neither seen nor heard anything, he went over to the Glenforsa Hotel and met David Howitt. The two of them then proceeded to search between the Glenforsa and Pennygown. This was a fairly small area, but from the approach the aircraft was making to the airstrip had seemed the most likely spot for the Cessna to come down on from the point it was last seen. This was also assuming it had not come down in the sea. They also searched the hill above Pennygown but neither search produced any trace of the plane or Gibbs. This search was a few hours after the Cessna's disappearance. By this time, the weather was bad with wind, sleet and rain, which continued for the following five days.

With the aid of maps and photos, MacLennan described the path of the Cessna, from taking off in a westerly direction, turning over Bowmore, and coming back down the sound before making a final turn to land, when it disappeared behind the trees. The two torches that had been used as supposed landing aids were also produced in the court. MacLennan had retrieved one of them himself and Frances Howitt had collected the other one from the strip.

MacLennan was asked how long it would have taken had Gibbs made a landing of some kind in the hills above the hotel and then tried to find his way back to Glenforsa? His response was that it would have taken a very long time. Quite apart from the appalling weather that had descended, the night was pitch black. On the terrain above the hotel, someone without a torch or light would have to proceed very slowly, so slowly that MacLennan said he doubted if he would even make one mile per hour. MacLennan was asked to describe a series of photos of the spot where the body was found. What the photos showed was the difficulty of finding Gibbs' body unless someone was to walk right up to it. The body was behind some trees, which seemed to suggest that Gibbs was looking for shelter from the wind and rain where he could rest. The wind was coming from the west that night and the trees had shielded the spot where Gibbs had lain down on the tree trunk.

MacLennan was asked if he thought it was possible the aircraft had come down in a forest, with two possibilities. One was not far from the spot where he was found and the other was 5 miles away and owned by the Forestry Commission. MacLennan agreed that Gibbs may have come down in one of the forests but added that they had fully searched the area of trees closest to where Gibbs' body was found. He added that, whilst they had searched the forest owned by the Forestry Commission there were areas of it that had not been checked because it was so dense. MacLennan was asked about Loch Bá, which was 4 miles from where the body was found. MacLennan did not say whether he may or may not have come down there but he did say that had Gibbs come down in Loch Bá and got ashore, he faced a 4-mile (6.4km) walk up a 1,000ft (305m) hill and during his trek in pitch darkness Gibbs would have had to cross a river in full spate. In addition to this, there were forestry fences he would have had to climb over whilst making his way on the rough ground. MacLennan said that a road ran alongside the river, which Gibbs would have had to cross in order to reach the spot where he died.

MacLennan also described two smaller lochs that were closer than Loch Bá to where Gibbs was found. These were much smaller than Loch Bá and one would have been too small (30 yards (27m) across) for a forced landing by the Cessna and the other, named Loch a'Mhaim, was marginal as to whether the Cessna could have come down on it as it was only 200 yards (183m) across. It would have needed Gibbs to make a very precise let down onto the surface in darkness (using landing lights) with high ground around. These two lochs were 1½ miles (2.4km) and 3 miles (4.8km) away respectively. MacLennan said that walking from these two lochs or Loch Bá, at the height he was at, Gibbs could have been guided by a flashing light at Lochaline across the Sound of Mull and also by the lights of Salen, which would have been on his left as he made his way towards the Glenforsa Hotel. The place where Gibbs' body was found would have been in a general line from the lochs to the hotel.

The lochs were peat lochs with silt at the bottom and somewhat surprisingly, when questioned, MacLennan said they had not been dragged during the searches for the missing aircraft. When asked why, he said that there was difficulty in getting the equipment up to the lochs as well as the difficulty in searching the lochs themselves. Once the water was disturbed, the peat and silt would rise. Another problem was that there was no real bottom to the lochs because of the silt and peat. There was also a number of lochans (small lochs) in the area, most of which were not very deep and composed of silt, but with rock underneath that.

With MacLennan's examination over, the next two witnesses were examined to provide some background to Gibbs' abilities as a pilot. The first was Anthony John Stone, who was an aircraft captain and knew Gibbs from the war. He had first met Gibbs in April 1945 and he had also flown with him from September to November 1969, so six full years before Gibbs died. His opinion of Gibbs' abilities as a pilot were that he was competent and had seen no reason to think otherwise. He also said that Gibbs did not strike him as a man who did things on impulse. Stone was only examined for a short period and in some respects was an odd choice to comment on Gibbs' airmanship considering it had been six years since he had flown with him and even then for just a short period.

The following witness was questioned extensively about his flying with Gibbs, but no mention was made of what his aviation background was, if any. This was Gibbs' business partner, James Rae. Rae was originally from the west of Scotland but was living in Teddington, Middlesex, and had met Gibbs in London three years previously. The two men had got on well and Rae described Gibbs as a 'loveable character' in evidence. The pair of them had gone into the building business together, focusing on structural joinery. They wanted to look for business in the west of Scotland with the possibility of using Mull as a base. Rae also had the intention of moving back to Scotland and leaving the London area. He did say that Gibbs was there on his final visit for a holiday only, not business, and that he had asked Rae to join him, but he had other commitments.

Rae said that Gibbs flew frequently and often hired aircraft from various people in different places. He also described Gibbs as being a good pilot and was 'very cool, calm and collected', as well as being cautious. Rae was then asked if there had been anything in their business that might have caused Gibbs some concern. Rae replied that he felt there was nothing that would have depressed him but that there had been a fire that had been a setback for the business. In response to this, Rae was asked if the fire would have depressed Gibbs enough to have made him behave as he did when he disappeared. He replied that it had been a matter for concern because the business had been affected and men they employed were out of work because of it. He did not feel that this would have depressed Gibbs to the extent that he would have recklessly endangered his life.

Turning back to flying, Rae described having flown with Gibbs numerous times, mainly to Glasgow (Abbotsinch Airport) and Prestwick. He had flown at night with Gibbs about half a dozen times and had also flown into the Glenforsa airstrip with him three times. However, they had not flown into Glenforsa at night. During one of these trips, Gibbs had commented to Rae that what the Glenforsa airstrip lacked was a beacon down the Sound of Mull to help with radio communications.

Rae's examination concluded with him agreeing that Gibbs was always confident when flying and that he never had any fears when accompanying him.

The person who followed Rae in giving evidence was probably the most important witness because she was the last person to see Gibbs just before he took off. Dr Felicity Grainger was a university lecturer living in London and had known Gibbs for two and a half years. She had flown regularly with Gibbs and they had visited Mull on a number of occasions, sometimes coming in by car and ferry. She said she had flown into Glenforsa with him on three occasions, and the last time before the final visit had been in October 1975. She said that she had no concerns about the way that Gibbs flew and described him as a cautious man and not foolhardy. When asked if Gibbs wore spectacles, she replied that she had never seen him wearing them, even for reading, and when asked if he had worn them when flying, she said she could not recall it.

She described the events of the final day and evening when Gibbs disappeared. She was asked how much alcohol Gibbs had consumed during the evening and whether he had consumed any whilst they were in Skye earlier that day. She said that she had consumed two glasses of whisky and two glasses of wine during the evening meal and Gibbs had drunk some wine but could not recall how much. She couldn't recall if Gibbs had taken any drink whilst they were on the Isle of Skye. The weather that evening, she said, was fine and fair with no rain.

Gibbs decided to go out to the Cessna at 9.30 p.m. after telling her that he wanted to test landing at the Glenforsa strip in case of an emergency at night. In response to three questions put to her: Did she discuss with Gibbs if it was a wise thing to do? Did she personally think it was a wise thing for Gibbs to do? Was she worried that he was going to test the strip at night? Grainger answered no to all three. Her negative answers, though, were given in the sense that she had not given any thought or consideration as to whether his flight might be dangerous. When asked by the court, Grainger said that Gibbs had told her he had done 'a lot of night flying' but she had only flown with him once at night when they had a problem with their aircraft's undercarriage and were diverted from Leicester to land at Luton.

On the evening that Gibbs disappeared, Grainger said that he had told her he was only going to take off and do one circuit and land. She had not expected it to take longer than five minutes. She then gave the details of the final minutes before Gibbs took off. In response to a question from the court, she said that Gibbs had not been wearing spectacles when he left. He was dressed in flying boots, cream trousers and a blue roll-neck sweater. In response to another question from the court as to whether she felt that he was adequately dressed for the conditions, she said that she thought it was alright as it was mild. They had walked the 50 yards (46m) from the hotel to the aircraft and both she and Gibbs got into the Cessna and he started the engine, leaving it running for five minutes. They taxied to the eastern end of the airstrip by the River Forsa, where Grainger said she got out and placed two torches to illuminate the end of the airstrip. Gibbs did not get out and Grainger stayed outside the aircraft and placed the torches on one of the two white runway header numerals. She could not recall if it was the '2' or the '6', and made her way over to the perimeter fence and Gibbs then took off.

She said he flew westerly then turned 180 degrees right to come back parallel to the airstrip, followed by two more right turns at the end to line up with the runway. It was at this point that Gibbs flew behind some trees beyond the eastern end of the runway and disappeared. From the moment the Cessna had left the ground to its final right turn to begin lining up to land and disappearing, Grainger estimated that no more than a few minutes had elapsed. She waited around ten minutes to see if the aircraft would reappear and during that time she heard no noise nor saw anything untoward that may have suggested the Cessna had crashed or come down. She did not see any lights when she looked over the Sound of Mull, although she was not far from the trees at the airstrip's eastern end, which obscured her view.

After the initial ten minutes of waiting, she began to feel uneasy and after twenty minutes, with no sign of the Cessna, she made her way back to the hotel to speak to the Howitt family who ran it. She described to the court how the police were contacted and calls made to Prestwick and Machrihanish. Around this time the weather eventually turned and it began to rain and sleet. Before she finished on the stand, Grainger was asked precisely when Gibbs had made his decision to take the aircraft up. She replied that she couldn't recall exactly, but it was the day before or the evening before. She stated it was not an impulsive decision.

The Howitt family managed the Glenforsa Hotel and following Grainger the next person to take the stand was Roger Howitt. He described Gibbs and Felicity Grainger arriving and booking in. Howitt had no flying experience himself but he confirmed that Gibbs had flown into the airstrip a couple of times before that he knew of. On the night Gibbs went missing, he had spoken to Gibbs outside the television room in the hotel around 8.30 p.m. and learned that he was about to take the Cessna up to test the 'night facilities for landing', as Gibbs had put it. Howitt said that he had seen Gibbs on the airstrip the previous day and he had spent more than an hour checking it out. Howitt had assumed that Gibbs was checking out the strip but he did not know then that he was going to make a night flight and landing. He described the weather on the night of the flight as poor with no stars, and it became bad very shortly after Gibbs had taken off and disappeared.

When questioned, Howitt said that although aircraft had flown into the strip in fading light before, he had no flying experience and felt it was not his place to tell Gibbs what to do. However, Howitt said he did show a certain amount of disapproval and mentioned that it would be wiser to use car headlights rather than torches to illuminate the airstrip. Gibbs must have felt what he was about to do carried an element of risk and that it was perhaps not very sensible because he asked Howitt not to tell anyone. When Howitt asked Gibbs who was he specifically not meant to tell and suggested his father, Gibbs replied that that would be OK but he didn't really want anyone else to know. Howitt finished the exchange with the fact that once the engine of the Cessna was started, everyone would know. When asked by the court if there were any scheduled night flights at the airstrip, Howitt replied that not only were there no scheduled flights at night, but even ambulance flights only used the airstrip during daylight hours.

When the Cessna's engine was started, Roger Howitt was in the hotel dining room when his brother rushed in and asked him if he had heard the Cessna starting its engine and asked what Gibbs was doing. Roger told him that he was taking the Cessna up, to which his brother replied that Gibbs was 'mad'. Roger, his wife and his sister-in-law then went up to the veranda of the television lounge on the first floor to watch, while his brother went to their mother's chalet overlooking the airstrip. He described hearing the engine running for quite a long time before the Cessna started to taxi. They watched as the Cessna taxied down to the end of the runway and although they could not see anyone, they did see the light from the two torches and the Cessna. When the Cessna failed to return, he said Felicity Grainger had returned to the hotel and with his wife then returned back to the runway with another torch. Grainger was very concerned as to what might have happened and they all felt that it was possible Gibbs had flown to Oban. After some time when nothing had been heard, Roger said they called the police and a search began. He looked in the wooded area beyond the runway and near the river, thinking that the Cessna may have crashed there, but he found nothing.

After the body was found on 21 April, Roger Howitt had confirmed Gibbs' identity in the mortuary and he also confirmed that the body was wearing the same clothes that he had seen Gibbs wearing before he went out to the aircraft on Christmas Eve. On the subject of the actual flight, Howitt said that the Cessna had taken off and turned towards Salen, before coming back down the Sound of Mull parallel to the airstrip and then making a final turn to come in for landing. Howitt had estimated the height of the Cessna at around 500ft and descending as it was coming in. He lost sight of it when it went behind the trees. After that moment, he said he saw nothing and he did not see any lights either.

Howitt was then asked by Ian Hamilton if he had received a phone call from him with regard to Gibbs, to which Howitt said he couldn't remember. Roger Howitt was followed by his brother David and he was asked if he had received the phone call from Ian Hamilton asking about Gibbs's competency as a pilot. David said he had not received the call either but was sure that it was his father who had taken it.

He said that on previous occasions he had seen Gibbs landing aircraft and he had struck him as a very competent pilot. On the night that Gibbs went missing, David said he had spoken briefly to Gibbs just after he had returned from Skye that afternoon. Gibbs did not say anything to him about taking the Cessna up that night. At 9.35 p.m. that night, he said he and his wife, Pauline, were watching the American TV detective series *Kojak* when they heard the engine being started and he watched as the Cessna taxied to the end of the runway. Howitt saw the two torches being adjusted but it was too dark to see anyone. He described the night as being dark with no moon and sleet starting to fall at five minutes to ten.

David confirmed the details of the flight in the same terms as the other witnesses. Gibbs had made a good take-off, flown towards Salen and then come back parallel to the airstrip at a height of between 300ft and 500ft, (91–152m) before turning to land and then disappearing behind the trees. He estimated that Gibbs was at a height of between 100ft to 200ft (30–60m) and was definitely descending as he turned at the near completion of his circuit.

David stated in a forthright manner that he considered what Gibbs had done as very hazardous and extremely foolhardy. When asked why, he explained that even as Gibbs accelerated down the runway, he thought he would ease off the power and stop before the end. He had assumed that Gibbs was only checking out the Cessna without actually taking off. Once he had taken off, David said he didn't see how Gibbs would have enough references on the ground to be able to make a safe landing.

About a minute or so after the Cessna disappeared, both David and his wife thought they had briefly seen a light on the Sound of Mull. They didn't know what this was and he said it could have been a trawler out in the Sound or brake lights on the other side. The light lasted for around fifteen to twenty seconds and he felt there was also the possibility that it could have been the Cessna. David had been looking through binoculars and he thought the light was orange in colour but his wife thought it was white. Neither David nor his wife could tell how far out the light was as it was so dark. He further explained that the light was to the north of the Cessna's path as it flew eastwards towards the base leg, before he would have made a right turn to line up for the runway.

Whilst David said the sighting may not have been the Cessna, he was concerned enough to go and get into his car and drive down to the runway threshold near Pennygown Cemetery using his car headlights and a torch to see if he could see anything. The trees at the end of the runway obscured most of the view of the sound and in addition to that, there were also Rowan trees there, which were not high but also partially blocked the view. David accepted that the light he had seen may well have been something else and he began to wonder if Gibbs had decided to head for Prestwick instead. When he returned to the hotel, he waited about another twenty-five minutes to see if the Cessna might return but then it began to rain and sleet heavily. Once the weather turned, David knew that Gibbs would not have been able to make a safe landing and, assuming he was still in the air, would be committed to diverting to Prestwick or Abbotsinch. On David's return to the hotel he met his sister-in-law coming back from the strip with Felicity Grainger, who was very upset by this point. David was surprised to see her as he had assumed she was in the aircraft with Gibbs. Grainger told him that Gibbs had a fuel reserve for approximately one and three-quarter hours' flying time. They waited for a while in case Gibbs phoned from Prestwick. When there was no call, they had no option but to inform the authorities and David first called Constable MacLennan. When MacLennan arrived, they searched the hill above Pennygown and the hill behind the hotel as well as the nearby farm. They also searched in the area where Gibbs may have undershot as he made an approach to the runway. This initial search was called off at 2.30 a.m. and they returned to the hotel. A group comprising of Grainger, MacLennan, Roger and David Howitt and his sister-in-law then went to the end of the runway where the torches were. They could see little there and the river was in full spate so David Howitt could not cross it, but they could see nothing in any event.

David confirmed to the FAI that he had been called up onto the hill in April to view Gibbs' body after it was found. He said that the clothes that Gibbs was wearing were the same as those he had on on the evening when he took off on his fateful flight.

David was followed on the stand by the shepherd, Donald John MacKinnon, who had found Gibbs' body on 21 April 1976. MacKinnon explained that although he had walked in the area numerous times before, he had not noticed the body for two reasons. The first was that he was preoccupied with the lambing season, which had just begun and took all his attention. The second reason was that the location was difficult to see unless you were close, from either underneath or above. MacKinnon said that you would need to be within 20 yards (18m) to see the body from above and that he, in fact, had actually walked past the body when he thought he had seen something odd and turned around to have another look.

The final witness was Strathclyde Police Inspector Douglas McCorquodale, who was stationed in Oban. The inspector had been in charge of the searches for the missing aircraft and pilot. He gave an overview of the case, including searches that were carried out in appalling weather that had included a helicopter, although its usefulness was hampered by the constant heavy rain, sleet and snow. There were also two Sea King helicopters involved in the searches over the Sound of Mull. It was McCorquodale's view that as there were no traces of salt water found on Gibbs' clothes, the Cessna had not come down in the sound. His view was that the weather was extremely cold and Gibbs would have been unlikely to survive the cold in the sea. He said that even if Gibbs had managed to swim ashore, he probably would have been unable to get to the spot where he was found, particularly as it involved crossing two roads, which he could have followed.

When questioned about the lochs in the hills, including Loch Bá specifically, the inspector said they had been observed from the air by helicopter and the nearby land had been searched on foot. He spoke of the difficulties involved in searching the bottoms of the lochs due to the soft peat and said that it was dangerous for divers. He also confirmed what had already been said by Constable MacLennan earlier, that the forests had been searched from the air and on the ground. Some parts were too dense to be searched on foot but these had been observed from helicopters above.

McCorquodale finished by saying that had Gibbs come down in one of the lochs, he would have had a long and exhausting trek over rough terrain, and a large part uphill, to reach the spot he was found in. He would have also had to cross a river in full spate as well.

The unanimous verdict of the jury was that Norman Peter Gibbs had taken off from Glenforsa airstrip on 24 December 1975 at approximately 9.20 p.m. in Cessna F.150H G-AVTN and did not return, and further, that on or about 25 December 1975, he died from exposure on the hill above Glenforsa airstrip. His body being found on 21 April 1976 was consistent with it having lain there since 25 December 1975 and no trace of the Cessna had been found.

There were two riders to the findings. The first was that Ian Hamilton was cleared of any blame or negligence, both personally and in relation to the aircraft. The second was that there should be no night flying undertaken from the Glenforsa airstrip.

Although the FAI had covered the events leading up to the disappearance of the Cessna, it gave no firm conclusions as to why Gibbs had flown the aircraft that night or what may have happened to it. Among some of the theories put forward are that there was more than one person with Gibbs (other than his companion, Felicity Grainger) when he took off. The suggestion was that the Cessna could have landed and Gibbs then got out before the aircraft took off again. Quite why Gibbs should go to all this trouble is not clear and even if someone else was flying, there was still the same problem with landing on Mull that Gibbs had. As part of this theory is the suggestion that there seemed to be more than one person moving the torches at the runway end before the Cessna took off. Grainger had said she was the only one placing the torches and giving evidence at the FAI, Roger Howitt made no mention of him, nor his wife and sister-in-law, seeing anyone else other than Gibbs and Grainger that night.

Another theory is that Gibbs had been working for MI5 and had flown to Northern Ireland to meet paramilitaries, who in turn had murdered Gibbs and placed his body where it was found above the Glenforsa Hotel later as a warning to other spies. While this seemed far-fetched, it would have been possible for Gibbs to fly to Northern Ireland from Mull, as the Cessna had enough fuel. In similar vein, another theory regarding Gibbs' odd behaviour in making the flight at that time of night was that he was involved in a jewel robbery that had taken place in Oban and the flight was necessary to help dispose of the loot. Both scenarios were plausible but at the same time they were sensational and it seemed like a lot of trouble for Gibbs to go to in each case when there were far easier ways to either meet paramilitaries or transport stolen jewellery.

What would make a conclusion easier would be to find the Cessna itself and bring it up. The actual location and its condition could give some indication of what may have happened. On 5 October 1976, an aircraft tyre and inner tube were found washed up to the north-west of the Glenforsa airstrip. They were found by a local farmer named Robert Duncan and were of the same type as those fitted on the Cessna 150, but it could not be confirmed if they had come from G-AVTN. However, the fact that they belonged to a Cessna 150 type was a strong indication they had come from the missing aircraft.

There were also a couple of reported sightings of the Cessna by divers. There has been some confusion over these as there have been a couple of discoveries of aircraft found in the waters around Mull that were thought to be G-AVTN. Two brothers named Richard and John Grieve, who were both commercial divers and members of the Glencoe Mountain Rescue Team, found what they believed was G-AVTN when they were diving in the Sound of Mull in September 1986. At around the same time, a local scallop diver named Bob Foster, who lived in a cottage on the shore at Lochaline, found what he thought was G-AVTN in 100ft (30m) of water in the Sound of Mull, roughly 300 to 500 yards (274–457m) offshore and a mile (1.6km) or so north of Glenforsa airstrip. There seemed to be some confusion over the different identifications. Richard Grieve had taken several photos of the wreck on his dive.

Whilst a definitive identification was not made without the wreckage being brought to the surface, the matter was further confused by three Royal Navy minesweepers that were carrying out a survey in early 2004 when they came across a plane wreck about a mile offshore from Oban. Again, the wreck was at a depth of around 100ft (30m) and it was assumed to be G-AVTN. An inspection by divers and a remotely operated vehicle

(ROV) showed it to be the wreckage of RAF PBY Consolidated Catalina (serial JX596) of 302 FTU (Ferry Training Unit), which had crashed on take-off with a South African crew on 12 April 1945. This highlighted the problem with aircraft wrecks in the sea near Mull. Oban was a very active seaplane base during the war with facilities in Oban, Ganavan Sands just to the north and the Isle of Kerrera offshore. A number of seaplanes crashed in the waters nearby between 1940 and 1945 and there are wrecks of five Catalinas (serials AH457, VA728, JX291, AH539 and JX596) and one Short Sunderland (serial N9022) in the waters off Oban.

So why would a man, who was described by many as a good pilot, even attempt to do what he did? With a bare minimum of night-flying experience, he took off from a strip that was totally ill-equipped for night-flying operations with an amateurish attempt at lighting, using handheld torches on a dark night with poor visibility and with bad weather approaching. His casual explanation to his companion, Felicity Grainger, that if he got into serious difficulties he would bring the wheels down into the water and after he got out he would swim ashore appear to be words spoken by either a drunk or someone who couldn't care less.

The plane did not even belong to him and, more to the point, he was not a young man, which might have gone some way to explain such foolhardy behaviour. He must have known that even if he escaped with his life, the issue with his licence would come to light in the event of an accident and loss of the plane. Although the insurance value was paid for the loss of the Cessna, there was a chance the insurance company could have refused to pay on the basis that he was technically not qualified to fly because of his invalid licence not being checked out properly. It would be expected that Gibbs must have had some inkling of this possibility and, again, the impression is that he didn't seem unduly perturbed at the prospect of causing the loss of someone else's property.

Could something have happened in his life where he didn't care what happened anymore? From the FAI and those who knew him well, there was nothing that was highlighted that could have been seen as something that would cause Gibbs to take his own life. The issue with the business mentioned by his business partner, James Rae, was described as merely a setback rather than some kind of cataclysmic event.

In order to try and understand why he made such a strange decision that night, it is helpful to look at what kind of a man Peter Gibbs was, along with his background. He had joined the RAF during the Second World War and flew Spitfire Mk XIIs with 41 Squadron. Gibbs joined the squadron in January 1944 at RAF Tangmere. By this time in the war, Germany was on the back foot and 41 Squadron was involved in patrols, providing escorts for bombers and attacking V1 sites. In March 1945, the squadron returned from Volkel in the Netherlands via Manston to Warmwell in Dorset for dive-bombing practice. On arrival at Warmwell on 18 March 1945, a number of the squadron pilots had completed their tours of duty and left, as did Gibbs, who left for 'medical reasons' that were not stated.

Gibbs was also an accomplished violinist and after he left the RAF, he formed his own quartet, the Peter Gibbs String Quartet, which was initially quite successful. Gibbs also played on a number of recordings for various record labels specialising in chamber music throughout the 1950s. In the numerous accounts of Gibbs' music career there is some error and misrepresentation. He was never a full member of the London Philharmonic Orchestra, nor the London Philharmonia Orchestra. He did play with the BBC Northern Ireland Orchestra and he led the BBC Scottish Symphony Orchestras from 1960 to 1963. Gibbs had also led the Orchestra of the Royal Opera House, Covent Garden, in the early 1970s.

The confusion over his being a member of the London Philharmonia Orchestra stems from the fact he was brought in at very late notice as a replacement for someone who had left. Gibbs joined the Philharmonia in May 1955 as the orchestra was about to undertake a tour in the USA with conductor Herbert von Karajan. There are numerous versions of what happened at the end of the US tour but basically Gibbs complained directly to the mercurial Karajan about his behaviour, which created a storm. What had happened was that the orchestra had played in a couple of venues that Karajan had felt were beneath his stature. At the end of these two concerts Karajan abruptly left when the applause started, leaving the orchestra to carry on sitting in their places during the applause. At the very least it was an ungracious thing to do and during the last rehearsal before they played in Boston, Gibbs stood up and firmly berated Karajan for his rude behaviour. Gibbs pointed out to Karajan that some of his friends had been at the previous concerts and had been offended by Karajan's abrupt departure from the stage. Gibbs finished by asking Karajan to apologise and then sat down. Karajan ignored the request to apologise and left. The eventual outcome was that, after their return, Karajan wanted a written apology from all members of the Philharmonia. This apology, which Karajan's solicitors had prepared, was returned unsigned and without comment. What this episode showed was that although Gibbs has been described in some accounts as an unassuming character, there are enough examples by people who had known him to show he was anything but.

Gibbs was a confident man. It could be said that he was overconfident. Although he obviously rubbed some people up the wrong way, he presumably saw himself as capable of dealing with most problems that life could throw at him. Many pilots who flew in the Second World War and survived came away with the feeling that they had escaped death or serious injury and avoided the worst that the enemy could throw at them. Peacetime flying, especially civil flying, was boring by comparison. An example of this is the problems experienced within British European Airways (BEA) in the 1960s with the former wartime pilots having reached positions of seniority in the state airline. There was some element of friction between these former wartime pilots and the younger pilots who had no experience of the war. The junior pilots referred to the older pilots as 'Bomber Buggers', whilst the older pilots would refer to the junior pilots as 'Milk Runners'.

This attitude of having survived the war led to a feeling of virtual invincibility in some pilots and in turn this engendered a lack of caution in airmanship. Gibbs was described by people who had flown with him as being quite thorough in his preparation and checks before taking an aircraft up. Ian Hamilton also described Gibbs in similar terms when he collected G-AVTN. However, Gibbs was also described by others as having a more nonchalant attitude during flying, with examples given of him flying under bridges and bringing his aircraft down to read road signs to establish his location, as well as once flying down to throw flower bombs at a bus being used by the London Symphony Orchestra. What may have contributed to Gibbs' possible overconfidence was the fact that he had already walked away from a crash. In October 1957, he had bought a DH.82A Tiger Moth registered G-APAW and had the storage area modified to fit his violin and case. Just over two years later, on 20 December 1959, the Tiger Moth suffered an engine failure as he was coming in to land at Redhill airfield. The subsequent crash damaged the Tiger Moth beyond repair, but apart from being shaken up, Gibbs was unharmed.

There are a number of things that contradict the image of Gibbs as being thorough in his airmanship and a cautious pilot. He had been less than truthful when he had told Felicity Grainger that he had done 'a lot of night flying'. It seemed odd that Gibbs would say this

The Glenforsa Cessna

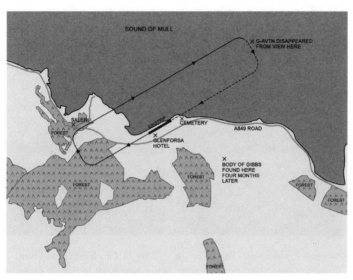

Glenforsa airstrip and surrounding locality showing the circuit of G-AVTN. (*bhardwaz – FIVERR*)

Cessna F.150H G-AVTN at Edinburgh Airport 4 April 1968. Gibbs had assisted with flight operations of the 12 AEF/ELUAS Chipmunks in the background hangar. He would have been oblivious to G-AVTN parked nearby, which would be involved in his death seven years later and 90 miles away. (*Dougie Martindale*)

Photo looking out over the Sound of Mull to the Glenforsa airstrip from Lochaline. The hills in the background show how hazardous night flying was in the area with only two torches on the ground to guide Gibbs. (*Calum Finnigan*)

G-AVTN on the seabed in the Sound of Mull. The full registration can be clearly seen. (*Richard Grieve*)

The upright of the 'T' and part of the 'N' can be seen here from the registration. (*Richard Grieve*)

The aircraft door can be seen just to the left of the centre of the photo. (*Richard Grieve*)

when the truth in his log book showed he had only completed five hours. Grainger had said nothing regarding her worrying about what he was about to do, so it suggests that by saying he had done a lot of night flying Gibbs may have had some doubts himself by exaggerating his experience.

Gibbs must have known that what he was doing was risky. His conversation with Roger Howitt before he took off suggests that he didn't want anyone to know about the flight, probably because it was foolhardy, not to say potentially dangerous. There can be little doubt that Gibbs viewed himself as a very competent pilot. So why then would he give the impression that he could comfortably manage a take-off and landing in the dark and then contradict himself almost by saying that if he got into difficulties, he would bring the wheels down in the water and swim ashore? It all points to Gibbs starting to display a lack of confidence in his ability to carry out the landing in the dark.

Another anomaly was the stipulation after his last medical that Gibbs would be required to wear spectacles whenever he was flying. For someone described as cautious and generally doing things 'by the book' it was a curious omission, especially as his last fateful flight was undertaken at night time when he would require good vision more so than during the day. His lack of spectacles would have been crucial with so few visual references at night.

Also, for a supposedly cautious man, Gibbs had not checked the forecast before departing and although Grainger had said it was mild when he took off, the weather was shortly to undergo a dramatic change for the worse. That wouldn't have mattered if he had arrived back within five minutes, but he had already mentioned the possibility of having to come down in the water. All these factors are the actions of a careless man, not a cautious one.

Gibbs seemed to have been a character who was either well liked or thoroughly disliked. During his time with the London Philharmonia Orchestra he was remembered by one member as being 'a strange man'.

Despite other very positive descriptions of Gibbs by some people who had known him, there was one place where he did not hit it off with everyone. During the 1960s, Gibbs had been playing with orchestras in Scotland and had done some flying out of Turnhouse (Edinburgh Airport), where he had been involved with the RAF 12 Air Experience Flight and Eastern Lowlands University Air Squadron (ELUAS). During this period he could often be seen over at Glasgow Airport (Abbotsinch) and frequented the Glasgow Flying Cub premises there. It has been said that he was a member of the club, but this is disputed by a former committee member from that time. He referred to Gibbs as being aloof and not mixing with other members of the Club, some of whom interpreted this offhand behaviour as arrogance.

Coming back to his fateful flight, there remains the possibility that Gibbs was well aware of his advancing years and the deterioration in his eyesight. That night was also the day before his fifty-fourth birthday. Was this, then, an impulsive challenge that he had set, to prove to himself that he was still at the top of his game in flying?

It was risky to fly there at night but Gibbs had flown into Glenforsa at least half a dozen times, as both Felicity Grainger and James Rae said they had accompanied him on three occasions each. He was therefore familiar with the airstrip and surrounding area. As he turned onto the base leg to start lining up for landing, he disappeared behind the trees at a height of between 300ft to 500ft (91–152m). Two things may have happened here. Due to a sudden disorientation caused by the trees obscuring the torches, Gibbs may have lost his awareness of his position and continued on a straight line on his base leg towards the high ground at 400ft (122m), which he would have only cleared by around 100ft (30m) or less. Travelling on further, he might have seen Loch Bá and decided it would be safer to slowly let himself down onto the surface. Alternatively, as he turned onto his base leg to line up for landing, with the loss of the visibility of the torches, Gibbs could have continued his turn and started heading back out over the Sound of Mull to try and fix his position by picking up the torches again. The significance of David Howitt and his wife briefly seeing a light on the Sound of Mull could have been the brief reappearance of the Cessna coming down into the water. Their sighting of the light was to the north of the Cessna's earlier path as it headed east.

Although it was stated at the FAI that the possibility of Gibbs coming down in the sea is unlikely because there were no traces of seawater or organisms in his clothes or in his watch, others have said that the higher layers of water in the Sound of Mull are less saline after periods of heavy rainfall. David Howitt accepted that he and his wife didn't know what the light was and he said it could have been a trawler out in the sound or car brake lights on the other side. Either way, Howitt had said that he could not have been sure it was the Cessna.

If Gibbs had come down in either Loch Bá or the Sound of Mull, an obvious question is why didn't he either call for help on the radio beforehand, and if he could not do that immediately, then why did he not climb to a safer height or get himself to a position where he could use the radio? Alternatively, why did he not call off the dangerous attempt to land at the Glenforsa strip and make his way to either Prestwick or Abbotsinch airports? Again the answer to this could lie in Gibbs testing his abilities. It would have been straightforward and simple for him to fly to either airport. There would, of course, have been the embarrassment of him having to explain why he had undertaken such a foolhardy escapade, but he would have been unharmed and the Cessna would have gone back to its owner. By either coming down on the sea or loch and making his way back to the Glenforsa Hotel, Gibbs was testing himself to the limit. The possibility that the Cessna came down in the area of forest is unlikely, despite the fact it was never fully searched due to its density in parts. Had Gibbs come down in a dense part of this forest, he almost certainly would have experienced greater injuries including broken bones, rather than just the cut on his leg. Also, if Gibbs had come down in this area of forest and if the police search parties were unable to penetrate it, it can be taken that Gibbs would have had the same problem trying to get out of it. His clothes would have had evidence of this as well (tears and marks and signs of vegetation), of which there was none.

Assuming the scenario that Gibbs had brought the Cessna down for a controlled let-down into Loch Bá, then swum ashore, he would have been soaked through on a cold, windy night and then begun what was, in effect, a 5½-mile obstacle course to get back to the Glenforsa Hotel. The first part would have been a long incline over rough and uneven ground, climbing over fences, with the terrain going up to a height of 1,000ft, and then the crossing of a strongly flowing river, which would have given him another thorough soaking. By this time, rain and sleet would have descended to add to his miserable situation. All of this would be undertaken in darkness without the aid of a torch.

It raises the question that if Gibbs had put the Cessna into Loch Bá and taken this route, then why did he not follow the road that ran alongside the river? Whilst his knowledge of the Mull landscape was unknown, it could have been that Gibbs had a rough idea of where he was, which was why he crossed over the river and continued on the rough ground heading towards where he thought the Glenforsa Hotel was. If he did not know where he was, it would have made more sense to follow the road, which would have made progress quicker and easier, and eventually would have led somewhere, or at least he may have come to a dwelling of some kind where he could have sought help. Quite possibly, Gibbs was also in a state of shock and not thinking straight. The clothes he was wearing would have been little protection once the weather deteriorated, plus the fact that he would have been soaked through. However, as long as he kept moving, he was relatively safe.

Whatever had happened to him, he was within a fairly short distance (just over a mile) of getting down the hill to the road that ran by the Glenforsa Hotel. If he had managed to stay alive until daybreak, he would have seen where he was and which way to go straight down to the hotel. It can only be assumed that he was so overcome by fatigue and cold that he had become disorientated and lay down to rest, which effectively sealed his fate. A victim of his own overconfidence.

As a postscript to this story, as the book was going to press, Richard Grieve kindly found and gave me the twenty-eight slides he took of the wreck in September 1986. Although some may say that they are not good enough to make a positive identification, to me they show the wreckage of Cessna F.150H G-AVTN and I have published on p. 56–7 three of them showing the full registration in one photo and a close-up of part of it in another, which shows the upright of the shape of the letter 'T' and most of the letter 'N' in 'G-AVTN'. On the basis of these photos, I believe Gibbs brought the Cessna down into the water on the Sound of Mull and made his way ashore. It was extremely cold and in a confused state Gibbs crossed the road and made his way up the hill, where his body was eventually found the following April.

I leave it to the reader to decide if this fits with their interpretation of what happened.

CHAPTER 2

THE KENNEDY CURSE

The Kennedy family need little introduction. The name has become iconic in US politics and synonymous with stylish living into the twenty-first century. Little introduction is also needed for the alleged curse that appears to have dogged a number of the extended family members. There is a long list of deaths and tragedies associated with a large number of the family.

Whether or not one believes in curses, the Kennedys have had more than their fair share of bad luck and tragedy. After the deaths of President John F. Kennedy in 1963 and Robert F. Kennedy in 1968, there were further deaths involving Robert Kennedy's children. Robert Kennedy had a total of eleven children. Of these, David Kennedy died aged 28 of a drug overdose in his suite at the Brazilian Court Hotel in Palm Beach, Florida, in 1984. His brother, Michael (both David and Michael were John F. Kennedy Jr's first cousins) also died in tragic circumstances. Michael Kennedy had been on a skiing holiday in Aspen, Colorado, with his family over the Christmas holiday period in 1997. On New Year's Eve he had been playing ski football with family members when he went head-first into a tree and suffered severe head and neck trauma. Despite attempts at resuscitation, he lapsed into a coma and died ninety minutes later in hospital. Ski football involves throwing a small American football around on a ski slope divided into fields, with the next goal being a tree or a sign. It is a game that some skiers consider dangerous to play and on this occasion Michael Kennedy lost control of one of his skis and could not avoid colliding with the tree. What had not helped matters was that they were playing in the late afternoon when many patches of well-skied snow turn to ice and it is thought Kennedy had hit such a patch and lost control. There was an official denial of a report that Michael Kennedy's brother, Max, had also been injured playing ski football on another occasion.

What is clear is that the Kennedys, as a group, seemed to enjoy taking physical risks and it was a trait that John Jr was to exhibit in a number of activities, often without any consideration for his own safety.

In respect of accidents related to the Kennedys, there are also a small number involving aircraft, which are less well known.

Joseph P. Kennedy Sr was the US ambassador to Great Britain from 1938 to 1940. Besides the tragic deaths of John and Robert and two of Robert's children, two other Kennedy children were to die in aircraft accidents. The eldest of Joseph Kennedy Sr's nine children was Joseph P. Kennedy Jr, who was to be widely tipped as a future Democratic leader and possible future US President. During the Second World War Joseph Kennedy Jr had trained as a naval pilot and after gaining his wings flew PB4Y-1 bombers on anti-submarine operations. The PB4Y-1 was basically a navalised B-24 Liberator bomber. Joseph Jr was posted to Britain in September 1943 and after two combat tours with a total of twenty-five missions under his belt, he was entitled to return home to the USA.

However, instead of taking the easy option that he had well earned, he volunteered for Operation Aphrodite. This operation, which was run by the US Army Air Corps, was extremely risky and Joseph Jr and his fellow lieutenant, Wilford John Willy, would be the first naval air crew to participate in Aphrodite's first naval mission. Kennedy and Willy were going to take off in a giant flying bomb and, when it was in the air, bale out once the guidance had taken over and it would then be steered onto U-boat pens in Heligoland. It was because it was considered so dangerous that volunteers were asked to come forward for these missions.

On 12 August 1944, they took off in a Liberator (a PB4Y-1 now designated a BQ-9) from RAF Fersfield, 16 miles (26km) south-west of Norwich, Norfolk. The aircraft was packed with 21,170lb (9,600kg) of Torpex explosive. Torpex is made up of 42 per cent RDX, 40 per cent TNT and 18 per cent powdered aluminium, and is 50 per cent more powerful than TNT by mass. Kennedy's aircraft was accompanied by two Lockheed Venturas acting as 'Mother' aircraft, a Boeing B-17 Flying Fortress acting as a navigation aircraft and a USAAF DH F-8 Mosquito, which was filming from its Perspex nose. Near the English coastline, Kennedy's Liberator made a remote-controlled turn at 2,000ft (609m). Kennedy and Willy then removed the safety pin to arm the explosives and he radioed the code signal

Spade Flush to indicate this had been done. They were the last words Kennedy was heard to speak.

It was to be several more minutes before Kennedy and Willy were due to bale out, close to RAF Manston, but two minutes after sending the radio message, there was a massive blast and the Liberator, along with both men, were obliterated. The explosives had detonated prematurely close to the village of Blythburgh in Suffolk. There was damage to several buildings on the ground and the Mosquito, which was flying 300yd (274m) behind and 300ft (274m) above the Liberator, was rocked and damaged by the blast. No trace of Kennedy or Willy was ever found.

For Joseph Kennedy Sr to lose his eldest son was tragic but perhaps understandable considering it was wartime and he was undertaking a hazardous mission flying what was basically a giant flying bomb. However, Kennedy Sr was to also lose his daughter just four years later in a civil accident, three years after the war ended.

Kathleen Kennedy Cavendish (John F. Kennedy's sister) had married William Cavendish, the Marquess of Hartington in May 1944. However, he was killed on active service in Belgium only four months later. Eventually she became romantically involved with Peter Wentworth-Fitzwilliam (the 8th Earl Fitzwilliam). On 13 May 1948, the couple were travelling to the south of France for a holiday. They boarded a DH.104 Dove, registered G-AJOU, belonging to Skyways of London. They were travelling from Croydon Airport to Cannes. The Dove stopped in Paris, where six passengers got off, and then resumed its onward journey. Near the Rhône River valley, just north of Marseille, the aircraft encountered a violent storm and plunged to the ground near Saint-Bauzile, near Privas, capital of the Ardèche department. Both Kennedy-Cavendish and Wentworth-Fitzwilliam, along with the two crew members, were killed.

This accident was far from the end of the Kennedys' involvement with aviation tragedy. Several years later, John F. Kennedy's brother, Edward, or Teddy, was almost killed in a crash on 19 June 1964 that killed the pilot and his aide, Edward Moss. The Aero Commander 680, registered N344S, was making an approach to Barnes Municipal Airport in West Massachusetts when it suddenly pitched into a steep climb, before crashing 3 miles (4.8km) short of the runway. Of the five on board, besides the pilot and Moss, Kennedy along with Indiana Senator Birch Bayh and his wife, all survived, with Bayh pulling the badly injured Kennedy from the wreckage. Although Kennedy escaped with his life, his injuries, especially a severe back injury, were to trouble him for the rest of his life.

Many years later, and although it was nowhere near as serious as the crash of the Aero Commander, Ted Kennedy was involved in another scare in 2006 when he was flying back to his home on Cape Cod after giving an address to the Massachusetts College of Liberal Arts. He was flying in a Cessna Citation 550 when the executive jet was hit by lightning and lost all electrical power and communications. The pilot managed to divert to New Haven, Connecticut, and make a safe landing.

Reviewing all of the above, it could certainly be argued that the Kennedys and planes didn't mix too well. However, despite this unfortunate track record, John Jr was attracted to flying, not just in a business sense by using a small aircraft to get himself around the country but also for leisure. He preferred to fly himself rather than using commercial flights for shorter journeys within the USA. His mother, Jackie, was deeply concerned by his seeming obsession with flying and did all she could to dissuade him. She had also seen, at first hand, the aftermath of an aviation tragedy. The event happened after she had married the Greek shipping tycoon Aristotle Onassis. His son, Alexander, was a qualified pilot who had also been killed in a flying accident when he crashed his personal amphibian aircraft, a Piaggio P.136L-2 registered SX-BDC, at Athens Hellinikon airport in January 1973. The fault was down to an incorrectly fitted connection in the controls.

John Jr was thrust into the public spotlight from the day his father was assassinated, just before his third birthday. The image of him saluting his father's coffin endeared him to the public and they never lost their fascination with him. After living on the Upper East Side of Manhattan in New York, when his mother married Onassis the family moved to live on the island of Skorpios for a time before returning to the USA. He attended Brown University, where he graduated with a degree in American Studies in 1983.

From the time he graduated to setting up his magazine in 1995, John Jr travelled abroad and tried his hand at a number of professions including acting, journalism and law. He failed his bar exam twice but passed on the third attempt and worked in the Manhattan district attorney's office for four years. John Jr also spent time doing his best to help those less fortunate than himself. Whatever might be said about the wealth that he was to inherit, he could just as easily have led an indolent playboy lifestyle. Among some of his undertakings were his involvement in heading up a non-profit group called Reaching Up, which was established to help people with disabilities to find work and open up opportunities for them. He also travelled to Guatemala to help with aid work after an earthquake there in 1976.

It was during this period of him trying his hand at various jobs that John Jr started to exhibit some of the more rambunctious aspects of his character. Some would say adventurous and others might say reckless. In 1992 he went with friends on a kayaking expedition to the Aland Islands in the Baltic Sea, roughly equidistant between Turku in Finland and Stockholm in Sweden. Kayaking in the sea, even between close islands, is hard work compared to kayaking on a river and John Jr went to the rescue of one of his friends, who had capsized.

Despite his gilded and enviable lifestyle, John Jr also had his fair share of concerns. One of them was the constant focus on his marriage by the media.

John Jr was a highly eligible bachelor and had gone out with a number of women in the public eye, including model Cindy Crawford and actresses Darryl Hannah, Sarah Jessica Parker and Brooke Shields. In 1992, he met Carolyn Bessette, a beautiful and sophisticated girl who in many ways was like his mother, Jackie Onassis. She was stylish and adopted a particular look that reminded people of the way Jackie had dressed. Carolyn had gone to Boston University and graduated with a degree in elementary education. She had tried a modelling career and eventually worked for Calvin Klein as the Director of Publicity for its flagship store in Manhattan, before becoming director of show productions.

Although publicity was her area of expertise, once she had started dating John Jr, the level of press intrusion and gossip was taken to another level. He had grown up with constant media scrutiny and was used to it. In fact, he had developed a certain rapport with the paparazzi and would regularly joke with them as they followed him around. Carolyn, however, was not used to being the subject of constant scrutiny from the moment she left her front door to the moment she returned, with hordes of cameramen camped on the doorstep. The constant attention was little more than harassment and there seemed little she could do about it other than leave her apartment at 7 a.m. every morning to try and avoid the worst of it. She left the Calvin Klein organisation in 1996 and in September of that year the couple married in secret on the remote Cumberland Island off the coast of Georgia. After their wedding, the media scrutiny got worse rather than better. The couple did their best to try and lead a normal life as best they could. Carolyn took up charity work as she felt that attempting to get any kind of a job she was interested in would lead to accusations that she was cashing in on her fame.

The constant intrusion eventually put a strain on their relationship and even their disagreements and arguments were subject to media scrutiny. They sought marriage counselling and by 1999 John Jr was living separately to Carolyn, who had stayed on in their apartment in Tribeca, New York.

John Jr also had another source of worry, which was a magazine he had helped to set up. The year before he married Carolyn, he had invested in a magazine named *George* (after George Washington), which had been launched in September 1995 but was not doing as well as he had hoped. The magazine was published by Hachette Filipacchi Media US and John Jr owned 50 per cent of the shares with Michael J. Berman. It was a glossy publication with a theme of politics allied to an upper-crust lifestyle with edgy themes, but it got off to a bumpy start when the cover of the first issue featured Cindy Crawford posing as George Washington, which attracted a lot of criticism. The aim was to make politics more accessible to a younger and wider audience by shedding some of its dry, staid image. However, the magazine struggled and Berman and John Jr had different ideas on the way forward. There were several rows between the two and eventually Berman left and sold his share. Sales continued to drop and at the time of John Jr's death the floundering fortunes of his magazine were a major concern to him.

John Jr's interest in flying extended to microlights and ultralights, which appealed to his adventurous nature. Only just over six weeks before the fateful flight, John Jr was hang-gliding at Martha's Vineyard when he crashed. He was shaken up and broke his foot, which required him to be in plaster for six weeks and use crutches to get around. While many people might have taken the shock of a crash like that and become a little more cautious about the dangers of flying, it did not seem to have concerned John Jr in any way other than the inconvenience of hobbling around on crutches. The cast was only removed on 15 July 1999, the day before he was due to fly up to Hyannis Port for the wedding of his cousin, Rory Kennedy. Despite the removal of the cast, his foot was still very tender and he continued to use the crutches.

In July 1999, John Jr's cousin Rory Kennedy was due to get married to a scriptwriter and author, Mark Bailey. Rory was the youngest of Robert F. Kennedy's eleven children and was born six months after her father's death. The wedding was to take place at the Kennedy Compound at Hyannis Port. The compound is actually three houses on 6 acres of waterfront property on Cape Cod by Nantucket Sound.

John Jr was exceptionally busy at this time and he had left travelling up for the wedding until the last possible moment. Although they were living apart at this time, he and Carolyn were still working through their problems and the two agreed to travel up to the wedding together in his Piper Saratoga. Also going to accompany them was Carolyn's older sister, Lauren Bessette. While plenty has been written about John Jr and Carolyn, not so much was known about Lauren. She had a twin sister in addition to Carolyn and after gaining an MBA she had returned from her studies to Morgan Stanley Investment Bank and spent four years with the company in Hong Kong. She was as accomplished as Carolyn and learned how to speak Mandarin Chinese. They were all close. Lauren also lived in Tribeca and was dating John Jr's cousin, Bobby Shriver. The plan was for them all to fly first to Martha's Vineyard, where they were going to drop off Lauren, and John Jr and Carolyn would then fly on to Hyannis Port for the wedding. Lauren had planned to meet Bobby Shriver in Martha's Vineyard that night.

On 16 July, an employee at Essex County Airport at Caldwell, New Jersey, made a phone call to John Kennedy Jr to check to see if he would need to fly his Piper Saratoga II that coming weekend. Kennedy confirmed that he would and that he intended to arrive at Essex County Airport between 5.30 p.m. and 6 p.m. that day, asking for his Saratoga to be made ready for that time. His original plan was to be at the airport for 6 p.m. at the latest and take off as soon as possible after that with Carolyn and Lauren. With that in mind, he could drop Lauren off in Martha's Vineyard and get to Cape Cod before sunset at 8.14 p.m. That way they would still have time to relax, have a few drinks and get ready for the wedding the following day.

Lauren travelled over to John's office with her gear and the two got ready to head out to the airport. Although John Jr had carefully planned out his busy day, he had considerably more to do than he thought and as a result he overran his time by a considerable margin. The sheer volume of traffic on the roads that late afternoon and early evening was also worse than usual, with the result he and Lauren did not reach Essex County Airport until 8.15 p.m. Carolyn arrived there just after John Jr and her sister. The employee who had phoned John Jr earlier that day had left the Saratoga fuelled up and ready to go outside the hangar, as requested by John Jr. Despite the fact that John Jr and Carolyn's marriage was under strain, they were putting on a united front for the wedding of his cousin. The presence of John Jr's sister-in-law, Lauren, on board the flight might have had a mediating influence should tensions arise between the married couple. Although John Jr had had his plaster cast removed the previous day, his foot was still tender and he was observed by witnesses at the airport that evening to be still using crutches to get around the apron. He was also seen to be loading the luggage into the Saratoga, despite the discomfort in his foot. The late arrival meant that by the time they were ready to depart, it was coming up to 8.30 p.m. and it would be dark by the time they landed at their destinations.

At 8.34 p.m. John Jr had started his engine and called the control tower for permission to taxi out for take-off. The Saratoga was given permission to taxi and to take off from the airport's runway 22. The tower asked John Jr if he was going towards Teterboro, New Jersey, to which he replied that he was going further north of it heading eastbound. The tower then instructed him to make a right downwind departure after take-off. John Jr confirmed the instruction and at 8.38 p.m. the Saratoga took off. The exchange between John Jr and the control tower regarding the departure was the last time air traffic control and the aircraft spoke to each other.

The Saratoga made a normal take-off and once airborne the aircraft was noted on radar a mile south of the airport at 1,300ft (396m) and heading north-east. By the time it had reached the Hudson River it was at 1,400ft (427m). When they had reached a point about 8 miles (12.9km) north-west of Westchester County Airport at White Plains, New York, it turned north over the Hudson River and John Jr put the Saratoga into a climb. After another 6 miles (9.6km), they turned east and continued to climb until they reached a height of 5,500ft (1,676m). From here they were on a course that would take them to Martha's Vineyard. They continued at the height of 5,500ft (1,676m) and passed just north of Bridgeport, Connecticut, passing the shoreline between Bridgeport and New Haven, Connecticut. After crossing the shoreline, the Saratoga continued just south and parallel to the Connecticut and Rhode Island shorelines. It passed Point Judith, Rhode Island, and went over Rhode Island Sound.

It was just after this that things started to go drastically wrong. When the aircraft was 34 miles (55km) out to the west of Martha's Vineyard, it started to descend from the height of 5,500ft (1,676m) that it had been maintaining. It was later estimated from radar that the Saratoga's rate of descent was between 400ft to 800ft (122–244m) a minute at a speed of 160 knots. The time was 9.38 p.m. and the aircraft had been airborne precisely one hour since take-off from Essex County Airport. While it was still descending, the Saratoga then began to make a right turn, heading in a southerly direction. Thirty seconds after making this turn, the aircraft stopped descending at a height of 2,200ft (670m). The Saratoga then began to climb for a short period lasting another thirty seconds. During this short period of climb, the aircraft stopped turning and its airspeed decreased to 153 knots. At 9.39 p.m. the aircraft levelled off at 2,500ft (762m) and flew in a south-easterly direction. This climb, cancellation of the turn, decrease in airspeed and levelling off, had all happened in the space of one minute.

Almost another minute after this, the aircraft made a left turn and climbed 100ft (30m) to 2,600ft (792m). As the aircraft continued turning left, it began to descend at a rate of 900ft (274m) per minute. The aircraft stopped its turn when it was facing an easterly direction but continued to descend at a rate of 900ft (274m) per minute. While still descending, the aircraft began to make a right turn and as it did this, the aircraft's speed and rate of descent started to increase rapidly. At its last recorded radar position just fifteen seconds after 9.40 p.m., the Saratoga was 1,100ft (335m) above the sea and descending at a rate that exceeded 4,700ft (1,433m) a minute. The impact with the sea killed all three instantly and the aircraft broke up and sank.

As nobody at Hyannis Port had expected John Jr and Carolyn to arrive at any particular time, the delay in their arrival was not noticed as people were preoccupied with the ongoing celebrations and preparations for the wedding the following day. The one place where the delay was noticed was at Martha's Vineyard Airport, where Lauren Bessette's friends were waiting to collect her. Their concern was all the greater because they were unaware that the Saratoga had left two hours later than planned. The airport at Martha's Vineyard closed at 10 p.m., although landing was still possible after this because it was possible to automatically activate the landing lights from aircraft coming in to land. By now Lauren's friends were so concerned at the non-appearance of the Saratoga that they asked a worker still at the airport to make enquiries about what may have happened. At the same time, they alerted Hyannis Port.

Senator Ted Kennedy was in his Washington home that night. He had been unable to get to Hyannis Port due to pressing business; he had been helping to push through legislation in the Senate to expand the Patients' Bill of Rights. He was told that John Jr's aircraft had failed to arrive at Martha's Vineyard. Once he had established that the Saratoga had definitely departed from Essex County Airport, he was able to use his not inconsiderable influence to start getting people out of bed to find out what had happened. Nevertheless, it was still well after midnight before any progress was made. By the time the Federal Aviation Administration (FAA) had confirmed that the Saratoga was not at Martha's Vineyard Airport and the US Coast Guard and the USAF Rescue Coordination Centre at Langley AFB had been alerted, it was coming up to 3 a.m. There was further delay because a check had to be made at all airports and airfields en route to rule out the aircraft landing at one of these because of the haze conditions that made night flying difficult. Coast Guard cutters set out to begin a sea search but because there was so little information available, they were almost searching blind in the hope of seeing something on the surface of the sea to give them a clue.

It was not until after daybreak the following morning that the search was given a major boost.

Early the following morning, President Bill Clinton was informed that John Jr and his aircraft were missing, along with his wife and sister-in-law. Clinton was also told that a search had begun in the area where the aircraft was believed to have disappeared. Clinton had long admired John Jr's father and he immediately authorised whatever federal resources could be used to assist in the search. Clinton came under criticism for basically allowing government funds (i.e. taxpayers' money) far above what would normally be used for the search of a small private aircraft that belonged to a person who was still a private citizen. To put it another way, Clinton had authorised the use of unlimited funds and resources on behalf of Joe Public, but no other member of the public would have received such largesse. Despite this, Clinton explained his decision by saying the Kennedy family occupied a special position in American public life. There was also huge public interest and the media gave a great deal of focus to the search. Besides Coast Guard aircraft and vessels, the US Navy and US Air Force also took part in the search. As if the air and sea search might be lacking in some way, the Central Intelligence Agency (CIA) deployed satellites over the search area to assist. On Monday, 19 July 1999, Clinton made the following statement, which summed up how many Americans felt about the developing tragedy:

As the search continues I want to express our family's support and offer our prayers and those of all Americans for John Kennedy Jr, his wife, Carolyn, her sister, Lauren, and to their fine families.

I also want to thank the Coast Guard and all those who have worked so hard in this endeavour.

For more than 40 years now, the Kennedy family has inspired Americans to public service, strengthened our faith in the future and moved our nation forward. Through it all they have suffered much and given more.

In recent years in particular John Kennedy Jr. and Carolyn have captured our imagination and won our affection. I will always be grateful for their kindnesses to Hillary and Chelsea and me.

At this difficult moment we hope the families of these three fine young people will feel the strength of God, the love of their friends and the prayers of their fellow citizens. Thank you.

Despite the heavy-duty back-up from the state to help in the search, the first indications that the Saratoga had crashed with the loss of all on board was when items began to be washed ashore. A wheel from the aircraft, Lauren Bessette's overnight bag with her name tag on it and a duffle bag were all recovered. This was followed by more parts of the aircraft and personal items washing ashore on Martha's Vineyard.

Back at Hyannis Port, the news of the tragedy led to the cancellation of the wedding. A tent that had been erected for the festivities was used instead to hold a Mass the following morning.

By the Sunday night, with more items washed up on Philbin Beach on Martha's Vineyard, there was still no sign of John Jr and the two passengers. Hope faded that they would be found alive after this period of time as they would have succumbed to hypothermia had they survived the crash.

The search area was narrowed down to an area of several square miles and divers were brought in. It was difficult work for the divers with the cold water, low visibility, strong currents and the threat from sharks. Four days after the accident, the point where the Saratoga hit the water was pinpointed and divers were sent to investigate at the location. The sea floor was around 115ft (35m) down but there was no sign of any debris. The sonar scans identified fourteen possible debris sites, all of which had to be investigated. Two Coast Guard vessels, the *Rude* and *Whiting*, along with the USS *Grasp*, concentrated on a narrow cluster of debris sites approximately five miles off the coast of Martha's Vineyard.

Eventually, very late on the night of Tuesday, 23 July, a remote-controlled underwater camera located the wrecked fuselage of the Saratoga lying upside down on the sea floor. By the following morning, the salvage and rescue vessel USS *Grasp* was over the point where the wreckage lay. The motto of the USS *Grasp* was 'Any Ocean, Any Time' and it had a formidable array of equipment and divers for this type of work. The divers went down first for a visual inspection and found John Jr still strapped in his seat in the aircraft cabin. The bodies of Carolyn and Lauren were found some distance away, also still strapped into their seats.

The force of the impact to the aircraft could be clearly seen as both wings had been ripped away from the fuselage and debris lay scattered in a line across an area approximately 120ft (36m) long. A 5-mile (8km) exclusion zone for aircraft and vessels was declared around the wreck site and the recovery of the bodies was watched by Ted Kennedy and his sons Ted Jr and Patrick. Once the bodies had been brought to the surface, the *Grasp*'s lifting gear then brought the fuselage up on to the ship's deck. Once the grim recovery was complete and thee autopsies were finished, it was agreed between the two families that the bodies of the three be cremated and scattered at sea near the crash site. A moving ceremony was duly held on 22 July 1999 and the ashes of the three were scattered from the deck of the US Navy destroyer USS *Briscoe*.

Even before the ashes had been scattered at sea, questions were already being asked about how the crash could have happened. There were many factors to consider. John Jr's capabilities as a pilot were examined in depth. From the time of first obtaining his private pilot's licence in April 1998 to his death, only fifteen months had elapsed. He was given a sign-off for a 'high-performance airplane' in June 1998. This was his single-engine Cessna 182. In May 1999, he was given a sign-off to fly a 'complex airplane', which was the Piper PA-32R-301 Saratoga II registered N9253N that he had bought from Air Bound Aviation Inc. of New Jersey. So in the short space of fifteen months since John Jr gained his original licence, he had advanced two further stages to more complex and higher-performance aircraft. Although they were all single-engine aircraft and he had gained the qualification to fly them in certain circumstances (i.e. he had not gained an instrument rating), he had not gained any depth of experience by building up his hours and flying in different conditions. In many ways, it could be compared to a learner driver who had recently passed his driving test and had rapidly worked his way up from a small underpowered saloon to a high-performance sports car.

His most recent logbook had disappeared with the crash but an examination of his earlier log, plus records from where he had trained, along with statements from instructors and pilots who had flown with him, were used to build up a picture of his total flying experience. What this showed was that he had accrued a total of 310 hours flying time, of which fifty-five hours were flying at night. Furthermore, the majority of his flying had been done whilst accompanied by a certified flying instructor (CFI). In other words, the total amount of flying he had completed on his own was only seventy-two hours. Even more significant was the fact that he had only spent thirty-six hours flying his Saratoga II and 9.4 of those had been at night, most of the time with an instructor on board. He had only flown the Saratoga II on his own for three hours and out of those three hours, 0.8 had been at night with one night landing. His experience on his own in this aircraft was therefore extremely limited, to put it mildly. What did stand somewhat in his favour was the fact that he had flown the route each way from either Essex County Airport or Teterboro Airport to Martha's Vineyard and or Hyannis Port and vice versa, a total of thirty-five times. He was at least reasonably familiar with the route, although many of the journeys were made in daylight hours.

Attention also focused on the injury to John Jr's foot from his hang-gliding accident. Despite his healing foot, following removal of the plaster cast the day before the fateful flight, he had received a FAA Federal Aviation Administration (FAA) Second Class Medical Certificate allowing him to fly. The fact that he was observed moving around the Saratoga on crutches before take-off and loading luggage points hints to an overly casual approach to the journey before him. It can be understood that having been immobilised for six weeks, he would be keen to get back into the swing of things, but the fact he was still using crutches shows he was uncomfortable without them. Most people would be happy to physically take it easy until an injury fully healed, but this behaviour seems to have been part of a Kennedy family trait; to throw themselves at life no matter what the consequences might be.

One of the main factors related to the accident was the weather that day and night. When the accident was being investigated by the National Transport Safety Board (NTSB), it interviewed three pilots who had all flown over Long Island Sound that day and evening. John Jr had flown under Visual Flight Rules (VFR) and the weather observations and forecasts were generally good and well above what was required. Whilst visibility was generally considered good by all three, there was a problem with the haze, and over water the horizon could not been seen. A fourth pilot who gave an interview to the news media said he had intended to fly from the same airport (Essex County) as John Jr to Martha's Vineyard that day but had decided against it because of haze. While three of the pilots had flown that day over the same area and another had chosen not to, they all mentioned the problem with haze. Had he been uncomfortable with the haze obscuring visibility, John Jr could still have opted to take a CFI with him for the journey to be on the safe side. He regularly flew with an instructor and one had made half a dozen flights with John Jr up to Martha's Vineyard in the same Saratoga. His opinion of John Jr's flying at night over the route was that he was competent enough in flying the aircraft and he also considered him to be cautious in his aviation decision-making. While that view of John Jr's flying does not necessarily tally with some of the decisions he made the night of the accident, it was a professional opinion of earlier flights he had made in the same aircraft on the same route. Significantly, another CFI who had flown with John Jr previously had said he was not ready for an instrument evaluation because he needed further training before he could fly the Saratoga on instruments. On the day of the accident, this CFI had offered to fly to Martha's Vineyard with him but was turned down by John Jr, who told him that, 'He wanted to do it alone.'

Another small issue was that although he was not officially required to file a flight plan, John Jr did not do so. By not doing this, it delayed the search slightly, although it would not have increased the chances of survival if he had done so. What it did do though was suggest someone who did not do things completely 'by the book'. None of these minor points were the proverbial 'deal breakers', but they all added up. Another matter that was commented on was John Jr's lack of communication on the flight after he took off from Essex County Airport. From the time of his last message to the control tower at Essex County Airport to the crash, John Jr made no attempt to communicate nor to monitor what was going on nearby his aircraft at any stage. This lack of communication and situational awareness was picked up in a TCAS alert close to Westchester County Airport. TCAS is Traffic Alert and Collision Avoidance System, which is used to reduce the incidence of mid-air collisions between aircraft.

At 8.49 p.m. a commercial airliner was making its approach for landing into Westchester County Airport when its TCAS alerted the crew to the presence of another aircraft in the immediate vicinity. The airliner was an American Airlines Fokker 100 operating Flight 1484 into Westchester County Airport. It was flying at

6,000ft (1,829m) and was instructed by air traffic control to descend to and maintain 3,000ft (914m). This was acknowledged by the American Airlines jet. The flight was then cleared to begin its approach to the airport, which again was acknowledged by the Fokker's pilot. There then followed an exchange between air traffic control and the American Airlines flight about the TCAS alert:

ATC: American fourteen eighty four traffic one o'clock and five miles eastbound two thousand four hundred, unverified, appears to be climbing.

AA Flight 1484: American fourteen eighty four we're looking.

ATC: Fourteen eighty four traffic one o'clock and uh three miles twenty eight hundred now, unverified.

AA Flight 1484: Um yes we have uh (unverified). I think we have him here American fourteen eighty four.

AA Flight 1484: I understand he's not in contact with you or anybody else.

ATC: Uh nope doesn't not talking to anybody.

AA Flight 1484: Seems to be climbing through uh thirty one hundred now we just got a traffic advisory here.

ATC: Uh that's what it looks like.

AA Flight 1484: Uh we just had a ...

ATC: American fourteen eighty four you can contact tower nineteen seventeen.

AA Flight 1484: Nineteen seven uh we had a resolution advisory seemed to be a single engine piper ... er ... Comanche or something.

ATC: Roger.

The exchange lasted two minutes and was more in the nature of making everyone aware of the presence of a light aircraft in the vicinity rather than any immediate danger regarding evasive action to be taken. The occurrence was outside the New York Class B and Westchester County Airport Class D airspace. Both of these categories of airspace require ATC permission to enter. The Saratoga was not within the airspace of either, but was close by. John Jr's presence had been noted by American Airlines Flight 1484, but whether he had noticed the airliner is doubtful. It was just one in a list of minor shortcomings that were starting to build up.

The Aircraft Owners and Pilots Association (AOPA) gave a list of reasons that would have all had some bearing on John Jr's abilities to fly that night. What was to feature strongly this day was the state of the weather. On the ground, it appeared to be a fine hot day but in the air, visibility was reduced because of a strong haze. The haze had affected visibility so much that a number of pilots had commented on it. One pilot who had just arrived at Essex County Airport noted that John Jr's Saratoga was being prepared to depart, so he went over to warn him. However, John Jr was at a convenience store near the airport buying some provisions for the journey so the opportunity of a warning was lost. The question has to be asked: Would John Jr have cancelled his flight because of a warning about severe haze? Considering his attitude towards risk, the answer would likely have been no, although he may well have considered delaying his departure to see if he could find an instructor to accompany him, despite his turning down an offer from an instructor earlier.

It has to be said, considering all the factors that John Jr had ignored (the weather, his injured foot, his lack of experience at night, flying without an instructor in difficult conditions) it all pointed to a belief that he would overcome all the handicaps facing him in flying that night. This arrogance alone with the risk taking, which seemed to be a family trait, was considered by many to be the flaw that sealed the fate of all three that night, rather than any one individual error John Jr had made. This could have been said to have been all well and good if he had just been risking his own life, but the fact remained that he had also risked the lives of his two passengers. Although the death of John Jr in the crash is what most remember about the tragedy, what tends to be forgotten is that the Bessettes lost two of their three daughters that night. The parents of Carolyn and Lauren filed a wrongful death lawsuit against the

Kennedy estate that was settled out of court in July 2001 for a sum reportedly in the region of $15 million.

In addition to the reasons mentioned, there were other factors to consider that all contributed to the pressures on John Jr that night. There was the pressure on him to always accomplish what he had set out to do, or in less formal terms, what was described by Dr Douglas Lonnstrom, as 'Get-there-itis'. It would have been particularly relevant in John Jr's case as he liked to push and challenge himself, whatever the odds.

Another factor that was mentioned in respect of John Jr's concentration that night was the fact that he and Carolyn had not been getting on well. At the time, they were living apart and attending marriage counselling, and it was felt that with the problems in their marriage John Jr may have had some difficulty in concentrating on flying tasks. It is, of course, an argument that could be used about many private, military and commercial pilots who might be having relationship difficulties. What exacerbated the problem in John Jr's case was the fact he was flying a more complex aircraft that he was still getting used to, and moreover he was flying at night in conditions that required his utmost concentration. The presence of Carolyn's sister would have helped to calm the situation as a third party present.

While a number of the reasons given as to what may have caused the crash can be explained away, one of the most puzzling aspects of what happened is why John Jr did not use his autopilot. The Saratoga II was equipped with a perfectly good one and had he used it, he would not have got into the difficulties he found himself in. It can only be speculated as to why he didn't use it.

It may have been egotistical, whereby he wanted to prove to himself that he was capable of mastering the situation without resorting to the autopilot, and possibly the element of risk involved.

There were lurid reports about the trauma suffered by the three in the aircraft. One gruesome photo claiming to be the body of John Jr on the deck of the USS *Grasp* after it had been brought up was proven to be false. Someone tried to cash in on the tragedy by trying to sell Carolyn's internet domain name. Still others tried to sell parts washed up from the crashed aircraft on eBay. One enterprising individual, in what must have been a real stretch, tried to sell seawater supposedly scooped up near Martha's Vineyard after the ceremony on the USS *Briscoe*. The selling point was that the water might have contained some of the ashes.

There has been much talk on internet forums as to why the three were cremated at sea instead of being buried on land, particularly in view of the fact that both families (the Kennedys and the Bessettes) were Catholics. A plot at Arlington cemetery had been authorised by President Clinton for John Jr and workers there actually went to the trouble of measuring it out and preparing it. However, there was more than John Jr to consider in the tragedy. The Bessette family also had a view on the funeral arrangements. It was agreed that John and Carolyn should not be separated and would be buried at the same place along with Lauren, which ruled out Arlington. A suggestion that they be buried at Brookline Cemetery in Boston, where other Kennedys, including John Jr's grandparents, were buried was ruled out because the Bessettes had no connection to the state.

The NTSB official accident report gave the most likely cause of the accident as pilot error due to spatial disorientation. However, a comment made by a *Vineyard Gazette* reporter in a TV interview caused some observers of the tragedy to look for other reasons for the crash. The reporter had said that he had seen a large white flash in the sky close to where the Saratoga crashed. While the reporter who made the comment could not later be found to verify the story, it set conspiracy theorists on the trail of what may have happened. One only has to look at the mass of conspiracy theories behind the death of John Jr's father and to a lesser extent, his uncle, Robert F. Kennedy, to set people thinking that there may have been a good reason why the crash of the Saratoga may not have been just a tragic accident.

One of the first possibilities looked at was a link to the crash of TWA flight 800. This Boeing 747 was on a scheduled flight to Rome via Paris with 230 passengers on board when it exploded off East Moriches, Long Island. This was further south than where the Saratoga came down, but still the same general area and it had happened three years previously almost exactly to the day. The cause of the crash of TWA Flight 800 was eventually found to be an explosion in the centre wing fuel tank but, as late as six months into the investigation, the NTSB chairman stated that the possibilities of a bomb, missile or mechanical failure as the cause were all still in consideration. If a bomb had been the cause of the crash of JFK Jr's Saratoga, not only would it be expected that there would be some evidence of it but it would also be expected that somebody would claim responsibility for the act. An accidental missile strike, whilst a possibility, is unlikely, as again there were no traces of explosive damage found. Having said that, there was always room for doubt, as shown in the TWA Flight 800 story, and other losses of aircraft have been suspected of being caused by them being shot down by missiles by accident.

There are numerous other theories but many are not fully supported in any way by what happened. For instance, one theory is that John Jr had committed suicide. While he had been known to suffer from depression and he was having problems with his magazine and his marriage, he gave no indication to anyone that he was depressed enough to take his own life and that of his wife and sister-in-law. The radar analysis of what the Saratoga was doing in the final minutes pointed more to him struggling to control the plane, and the corkscrewing effect of the aircraft spiralling downwards fits more with a scenario of what is known as a 'graveyard spiral' where the pilot has lost the horizon and lost control of the aircraft. Tied in with the suicide theory is one that John Jr had faked his own death in order to fight the 'Deep State' who had organised the killing of his father and his uncle and would probably look to kill him as well. Quite how he would fight back against the Deep State is not known and he would need a lot of help. At the time of writing it is approaching twenty years since the accident and there has been no evidence that John Jr is still alive, or indeed any evidence of his making any fight against the Deep State. Also, both his wife Carolyn and her sister Lauren would also have had to have disappeared, given there has been no sight of them since.

A variation on the Deep State theory is that John Jr was killed because he was going to publish in his magazine

John Kenndy Jr

A Piper Saratoga II similar to the one flown by John F. Kennedy Jr on 16 July 1999. (*John Coleman/ABPIC*)

John F. Kennedy Jr and his wife, Carolyn. (*Courtesy JFK Presidential Library & Museum, Boston*)

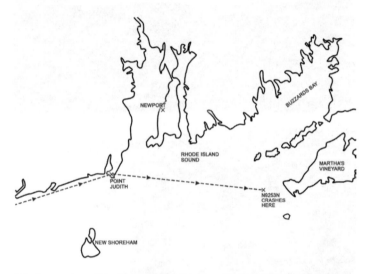

The last section of the flight of John Jr's Piper Saratoga II before it came down in the sea. (*bhardwaz – FIVERR*)

George who was really behind the assassination of his father. This theory, published on the internet, states the involvement of no less a person than President George H.W. Bush, who, it is alleged, had close links to the CIA at the time of President John F. Kennedy's assassination. The theory alleges that even the name of his magazine *George* is an allusion to who John Jr believes was involved in the killing of his father.

Besides the suggestion that John Jr deliberately crashed the Saratoga to commit suicide, another theory that was published in the *Globe* on 15 June 2009 has him crashing the aircraft because he was suffering from Attention Deficit Disorder (ADD) as well as dyslexia.

In an article published in October 2009, another theorist, a Canadian-born Israeli writer named Barry Chamish, put forward his dramatic suggestion that John Jr was murdered by Israeli operatives because he was about to publish an explosive exposé in his magazine *George* on who had really killed Israeli Prime Minister Yitzhak Rabin. John Jr's magazine had already run a story about the murder of Rabin in its March 1997 edition, but the new article was intended to be far more revealing.

Rabin had been assassinated in Tel Aviv on 4 November 1995 by an Israeli ultra-nationalist who opposed his peace initiatives and the signing of the Oslo Accords, which were intended to lead to the Palestinian right to self-determination. Chamish, who died in 2016, had published a book entitled *Who Murdered Yitzhak Rabin?* In it he explained that the original reports of the FBI and the FAA suggested foul play in John Jr's death and that they had been suppressed and substituted with a story about bad weather and problems with Kennedy's foot. The imminent arrival of the then current Israeli Prime Minister, Ehud Barak, for a meeting with President Bill Clinton, gave some urgency to stopping the exposé by John Jr in his magazine. This article was to explain who was behind Yitzhak Rabin's murder, and therefore the Israeli government could not allow it to be published, or so the reasoning went.

Chamish went on to allege that the Saratoga had been destroyed by a bomb planted in the tail section of the aircraft. As if this was not hard to believe already, he then goes on to say that Hillary Rodham Clinton was also involved and that her husband, Bill Clinton, basically got the US Navy to cover up the crime. It is a suggestion that is as preposterous as it sounds. The reason the Clintons were supposedly involved was because John Jr was planning to run for the New York Senate seat that Hillary Clinton was interested in running for. To summarise: The murder of John Jr would therefore not only stop the revelation of the 'truth' behind Yitzhak Rabin's murder but an added, alleged, benefit was that Hillary Clinton would have no opposition for her Senate seat and her husband could use the US Navy to cover up the crime.

Whether or not it is believed that one of the numerous theories is true and that John Jr had fallen victim to nefarious dealings involving the Deep State, or had fallen victim to ADD or committed suicide, the fact is that he was the latest in a long line of Kennedys to suffer bad luck. It has been said that bad luck can come from deep inside a person. If that bad luck was deep within John Jr, coupled with his carefree attitude towards his own safety, it was only a matter of time before he met his tragic end.

CHAPTER 3

THE KINROSS INCIDENT

In the early evening of Monday, 23 November 1953, a radar operator was working his shift at the USAF Naples Ground Control Interception (GCI) radar station. The Naples station was part of a group of five in the Lake Superior region, Canada, and was located just south of the Sault Ste. Marie locks system on the eastern side of Lake Superior. As he was looking at his screen that evening, he noticed an unidentified radar blip making its way across Lake Superior towards the area of the shipping locks at Sault Ste. Marie. The blip that had appeared on his radar screen was approximately 160 miles (258km) to the north-west of Kinross Air Force Base, which was close to the Naples radar station. The unidentified aircraft, or bogey as they were known, had come out from over land and into the air space above the lake at a height of 7,000ft (2,134m). More importantly, the unidentified radar contact was flying in a direction that could take it towards the restricted air space above the locks at Sault Ste. Marie and had made no attempt to identify itself. The Naples station was part of the chain of air defences looking towards the northern polar region from which an attack by bombers from the Soviet Union would be expected to come. Whilst a solitary blip did not represent an attack by hordes of Soviet bombers, it was nevertheless of concern because it could not be identified.

The operator continued to watch as the blip continued in a south-easterly direction, still maintaining its height of 7,000ft (2,134m). Because the operator was unable to identify it, he logged the blip as 'Unknown' and activated the alert system for an interceptor to investigate the bogey. Kinross Air Force Base was close to the locks at Sault Ste. Marie and was the nearest base for interceptors. That night two aircraft from the 433rd Fighter Interception Squadron (FIS) were in residence. The detachment of two aircraft had come over to Kinross from their home base at Truax Field near Madison, Wisconsin, to replace the usual residents (438th FIS) for a short period while they were at Yuma, Arizona, undergoing gunnery training. Kinross was a base that stood guard ready to intercept any incoming bomber attack coming from the north from the Soviet Union over Canada and into the USA. As the operator continued watching the blip head across Lake Superior, confirmation was received that it could not be identified and an interceptor sprang into action.

There were two, two-man, alert crews at Kinross Air Base both on standby, ready to go into action in their Northrop F-89C Scorpion fighters. The second crew were ready to take to the air in a thirty-minute time frame. The faster of the two crews were ready to fly on only five minutes' notice. The crew on the shorter alert were sitting in the alert room occupying themselves the way alert crews all over the USA did at that time, by playing games such as gin rummy, reading, listening to music and watching television. The facilities were comfortable and the food was always good. The aircraft for the five-minute alert was serial 51-5853. The Scorpion was one of the post-war generation of interceptors that appeared to be a design hybrid of the fastest and most agile of the later propeller fighters like the P-51 Mustang but incorporated lessons learned from the first jet fighters. They all had in common large straight wings, with the Scorpion being distinct on account of its swept-up tail, giving a menacing appearance with its tail in the air ready to sting. Tom McCarthy, a former Scorpion pilot, gave his view of the aircraft and sitting on alert:

> The airplane had a real ergonomically nice cockpit with plenty of room and a nice instrument flying layout, good because we flew in some nasty weather when other fighters did not. The D was a bit underpowered but handled well and was easy to land since it had a nice wide landing gear. We flew the J at higher airspeeds and it was better handling.
>
> Sitting alert was not boring as the facilities were normally well equipped, comfortable, good food, usually 4 good guys and always TV and good reading material. The early 89s experienced a number of wing failures ... but they were fixed by the time I flew the a/c. The 89 airscoops were fairly close to the ground and required screens at times. We called it the Hoover vacuum cleaner. Comparing it to others is not really fair, it did what it was supposed to do ...

Once the Alert horn was sounded, the crew on the short alert, 1st Lt Felix Moncla Jr and 2nd Lt Robert Wilson, ran out to the Scorpion in the alert hangar, climbed in, started the engines and taxied out to the runway. At 1822hrs (EST), Moncla turned on the afterburners. The Scorpion thundered down Kinross's runway and leapt into the sky. Moncla put the aircraft onto a north-westerly heading and started climbing to 30,000ft (9,144m). Nine minutes after take-off, radar control of the Scorpion was transferred from Naples to Pillow radar station to continue the interception. The radar operator at Pillow was USAF 2nd Lt Douglas Stuart and he now began to give instructions to Moncla. Once the Scorpion reached 30,000ft (9,144m), it was vectored towards the unidentified radar contact and at 1847hrs EST the interceptor was instructed by Pillow GCI to descend to 7,000ft (2,134m) and prepare for the interception. Moncla took the Scorpion down to 7,000ft and was then given a further instruction by Stuart to make a turn on a heading of 20 degrees, which would take the Scorpion directly to the vector cut-off. Once Moncla had made the turn, he was informed by Stuart that the unidentified aircraft was at 11 o'clock and 10 miles (16km) away from him. It was a dark night and visibility was poor. During the time that the Scorpion was being vectored to intercept the bogey, it had not deviated from its course or changed height, which had maintained at 7,000ft. On Pillow's radar scope, Stuart watched closely as the radar returns from the two aircraft approached each other and then merged into one. Then the unidentified aircraft radar blip continued on its original course without any deviation. The Scorpion had disappeared from the screen and it was not just the radar return that had gone, the aircraft itself had completely disappeared. The last radio contact with the interceptor had been at 1852hrs EST.

The weather that night was far from ideal. An area of low pressure was centred over northern Minnesota and was moving eastwards towards Lake Superior. A cold front extended south through central Minnesota, Iowa and eastern Kansas, and in the local area where the Scorpion had gone missing, there was a fresh south-westerly flow ahead of the approaching cold front. The eastern half of Lake Superior was overcast with stratocumulus clouds with a base of around 2,000ft (609m) going up to 3,000ft (914m) further east towards Sault Ste. Marie. Above this was a second layer of alto stratus cloud extending up to 14,000ft (4,266m) from a base of around 8,000ft (2,438m) in the western part extending up to 10,000ft (3,048m) heading towards Sault Ste. Marie. Above the alto stratus was yet another layer of scattered cirrus cloud at 18,000ft to 20,000ft (5,486–6,096m). Despite the amount of cloud around, there was moderate visibility of between 8 and 10 miles over the whole area; what was really reducing visibility was the presence of isolated snow showers. Although these were relatively light, they were over the whole area in patches and bringing the cloud base down as low as 500ft (152m), reducing visibility to 1 to 2 miles (1.6–3.2km). A further complication was that radiosondes (weather balloons transmitting data) taken at 1630hrs at Sault Ste. Marie were reporting moderate to heavy icing in all clouds. The air was stable with little or no turbulence, suggesting that rime icing would form in the clouds. Rime icing is formed by super-cooled droplets of water which freeze on impact.

This increases drag and decreases the ability of the airfoil to create lift. Combined with low temperatures of minus 5 degrees at 5,000ft (1,524m), down to minus 25 degrees at 20,000ft (6,096m), the poor weather was to have a considerable bearing on search and rescue efforts.

Once the Scorpion had disappeared from the radar screen and was not responding to any messages, a full search and rescue operation got under way. The 49th Air Rescue Squadron based at Selfridge Air Force Base alerted the Eastern Area Radar Control Centre (RCC) at 2200hrs that an F-89C fighter had gone down northwest of Sault Ste. Marie. It was pointed out that the only emergency equipment carried by the crew was a one-man dinghy each for Moncla and Wilson. Considering the extreme cold, it was vital that if Moncla and Wilson had come down on Lake Superior and managed to get into their dinghies, they be found as quickly as possible. The radio and radar contact with the Scorpion had been lost at position 4800N 8649W and just prior to this Moncla had received and acknowledged an instruction to steer to base of 150 degrees T (true heading as opposed to magnetic heading) and a new track to fly of 020 degrees magnetic. One problem some early interceptors had was a lack of fuel capacity, with a subsequent inability to stay in the air too long, or loiter. However, this was not the case with the Scorpion as 51-5853 had enough fuel on take-off to stay in the air for one hour and forty-five minutes. At the time contact was lost, it had only been in the air for just under half an hour, so fuel was not an issue.

The normal communications checks were carried out by the 49th Air Rescue Squadron but these came up negative. Over on the Canadian side, the Ontario Provincial Police had been alerted. Information had been placed with radio stations in Sault Ste. Marie, Ontario, on the northern side and Sault Ste. Marie, Michigan on the southern side, along with the Ontario Department of Lands and Forests, which made a communications check of its own radio stations in the area where it was believed the Scorpion could possibly have come down. All these checks came back negative.

A search HQ was set up at Kinross Air Force Base at 1215hrs EST the day after the disappearance. It was a joint effort with the Canadians, who gave every assistance they could. The searchmaster was Flt Lt Campbell, who came over from RCAF (Royal Canadian Air Force) 102 C&R Flight at Trenton. His assistant was Flg Off B. Ketcheson, who had arrived earlier to work with the USAF team. Prior to the arrival of the RCAF searchmaster, USAF Captain Meyer had arrived at Kinross from Selfridge Air Force Base to act as liaison officer. He acted in this role until 26 November, when he was replaced by another officer from Selfridge Air Base, Captain Davenport, who was to remain at Kinross till the end of the search. Between them they came up with a search plan that combined ships and aircraft to expand on the immediate search that had been undertaken on the night the Scorpion disappeared. The US Coast Guard had provided a vessel and an SA-16 Albatross and the 49th Air Rescue Squadron provided two SA-16s. The Albatross was a twin-engine amphibian that had been designed to operate in large areas of ocean in the search and rescue role. It could land in rough seas with waves up to 4ft (1.2m) and was ideal to undertake the search for the missing fighter jet.

In addition to ground contact being maintained with stations at Houghton, Grand Marie and Sault Ste. Marie, there was good ground communication with the Canadians as well with W/T (Wireless Telegraphy) and R/T (Radio Telephone) contact maintained with the Ontario Department of Lands and Forests' ground stations. The initial three aircraft and surface vessel had proceeded immediately to the vicinity of 4800N 8649W, where the Scorpion was believed to have gone down. Once there, they began an expanding search block that continued through the night of 23/24 November and well into the next day. The continuing appalling weather stopped the searchmaster sending out any more aircraft. This difficulty was compounded by the unknown position of one of the SA-16s that was still searching a box area. Although a search had been carried out on the night the Scorpion disappeared, the weather was so bad that no further night searches were undertaken. A grim factor in making this decision was the potential survivability of Moncla and Wilson in the freezing conditions with only minimal survival equipment.

Initially, the search boxes were laid out to cover a distance of 60 miles (96km) west (towards Sault Ste. Marie) of the last reported position of the Scorpion. The remaining squares were in the area located to the east of the last known position. In addition to these search areas, Scorpion crews at Kinross had been interviewed for their views on the disappearance and the consensus of opinion was that at the first sign of trouble they would have turned on the homing device at 150 degrees, which Moncla had confirmed he was turning onto. Taking this information into account, the searchmaster established further search blocks out to the south, east and south-east. With a 2-mile (3.2km) visibility on average, the aircraft searched the blocks from a height of 1,000ft (304m). In addition to the search blocks, the aircraft also searched the coastline of Lake Superior from a height of 500ft (152m) with half a mile visibility. The coastline searched was along the east and north shore of the lake from Sault Ste. Marie taking in Simpson Island Marquette.

There was no improvement in the weather during the search period. The constant low cloud base and reduction in visibility made things very difficult for the search crews. On the afternoon of 25 November and the morning of 26 November there was heavy icing on the search aircraft, which led to lengthy delays in getting airborne whilst they were being de-iced.

Despite the resources that were put into the search, only 80 per cent coverage of the search area had been achieved within the time frame allowed for the search. The USAF had committed an H-15 helicopter, a C-47 and a C-45 from Kinross; two Albatrosses, a B-25 and a C-45 from Selfridge Air Force Base plus two C-45s from the USAF facility at Chicago's O'Hare Airport. The US Coast Guard provided the vessel USCG *Woodrush* from Sault Ste. Marie, along with two of its Albatrosses from Traverse City and finally the RCAF had sent three C-47s from Centralia Air Force Base and another C-47 from the RCAF base at Trenton. In addition to the military and Coast Guard, there was also participation from four Cessna 140 light aircraft from the Civilian Air Patrol at Sault Ste. Marie. So, a total of 29,600 square miles (76,664 square km)was searched in just over 143 hours of search flying time by eighteen aircraft, a helicopter and a Coast Guard Cutter with not a single trace of the missing Scorpion and its crew. It would be expected that had the Scorpion hit the waters of Lake Superior at high speed, it would have broken apart and there would be some items at the very least found floating in the water. However, there was nothing. Land searches were also conducted, but these were hampered by heavy snow.

During the search, a number of leads came in including a radio transmission that was overheard discussing plane wreckage. When this was investigated, it was traced to South Bend, Indiana, and involved a search for a completely different missing aircraft. The wreckage of this other missing aircraft was eventually found in that area. Apart from this, there were two other promising leads. The first was reported on 25 November 1953 when a post carrier had reported seeing what he thought was the wreckage of an aircraft in the water in the Cut River Bridge area (455730N 8457W). The Michigan State Police searched the area three times and eventually concluded that the post carrier had seen rocks in the water. The other lead was the reported sighting of aircraft wreckage on the side of a mountain about 80 miles north of Kinross Air Force Base. Three aircraft (a C–47, a C–45 and a B–25) and a helicopter were allotted to search this location, which they did extensively, but nothing was found. Hope had faded for the missing aircrew and after a review of operations, it was decided to suspend the search on the evening of 28 November 1953, five days after the disappearance of the Scorpion.

Apart from the fate of the missing fighter and its crew, the big question was: what was the mystery blip? It turned out that at the time of the Scorpion intercept, an RCAF C-47, serial VC-912 (the actual serial was 10912 and 'VC' denoted Canada). VC-912 had taken off from Winnipeg and was heading for the RCAF Air Base at Sudbury. It was believed to be flying off course and was at 7,000ft (2,134m). What had drawn attention to this aircraft was its route over the restricted air space over the Sault Ste. Marie locks, heading out over northern Lake Superior in a direction west to east that would take it over the locks. However, the commander of this aircraft, Captain Gerald Fosberg, had stated quite clearly that not only had he not seen the Scorpion, but he was also adamant that he was not off course either and was flying west to east towards RCAF Sudbury Air Base on a line that was 30 miles north of the blip over Lake Superior. Whatever had happened between the Scorpion and the blip, they had literally merged together on the radar screen and were both at the same height, which suggested they must have passed extremely close to each other, possibly causing one of them to take evasive action. The mystery blip did not alter its course and carried straight on, so even if the Scorpion had taken violent evasive action, possibly going into a steep and uncontrollable dive, it still would have shown on the radar screen after they had merged. The USAF concluded that the mystery blip must have been the RCAF C-47 which had taken off earlier from Winnipeg. However, no definitive proof was provided in their accident investigation, which would suggest that the blip was tracked to Sudbury, nor indeed any clarification on what became of the mysterious blip. After Fosberg had landed at Sudbury, he received a phone call asking him if he had seen anything on his flight and he replied that he had not. There were no marks of any kind on the C-47, so even if it had met the Scorpion and the crew had not seen it, there was no glancing blow anywhere on the C-47 to suggest it had struck the Scorpion and sent it out of control unbeknownst to the Canadian crew. It is highly unlikely the crew of the Canadian aircraft would not have noticed even a slight collision of some kind.

The Scorpion was an aircraft that did not have a great reputation to start with. This was due to a number of crashes after it came into service, including one highly public accident during a display on 30 August 1952 at Detroit Airport that killed the pilot and the radar observer. The problem was identified as a weakness in the wing root and the airshow manoeuvring led to a catastrophic failure causing the wing to break off. Over a period of time, the entire fleet of Interceptors was grounded until the problem was identified and then rectified. All the Scorpions currently in service at the time were put through an extensive modification programme, with the wing roots strengthened and a fin was added to the wingtip tanks to stop the 'flutter' that was creating stress on the wings. Scorpion 51-5853 had already had the work completed, so the weakened wing roots were not a factor in what might have happened to the aircraft.

With regard to any other possible mechanical issues, the maintenance report for the missing Scorpion showed that it was given a thorough preflight inspection at 0730hrs that morning and there were no issues found. The Scorpion was launched on an earlier scramble at 1145hrs and returned exactly an hour later at 1245hrs. The pilot had filled in the AF Form I (this was a post-flight form to report any problems) and had noted in the remarks 'Flt #1 OK'. Scorpion 51-5853 was then given a service and spot checked for worn tyres, clear engine intakes, oil and hydraulic tank levels, plus the oxygen and nitrogen were checked. The maintenance crew then replaced all the servicing caps and covers on the aircraft and it was towed back into the alert hangar, where it was returned to duty as the number one aircraft on a five-minute alert status. The maintenance report stated that the aircraft was again scrambled at 1815hrs (on its fateful flight) and stated that there had been no issues or difficulties before it took off. A clean bill of health and any earlier problems resolved does not mean to say that there was not some catastrophic failure in the aircraft during the interception, but without finding the wreckage there remains no way of knowing.

The other area considered was a problem involving one or both crew members blacking out. Felix Moncla had accrued a total of 811 hours' flying time and it was said that he suffered from vertigo. One theory is that Moncla's vertigo came on at the time of the interception whilst the aircraft was making an extreme manoeuvre and he became badly disorientated, losing control of the Scorpion. If it was the case that Moncla genuinely had suffered from vertigo and it came on during a difficult manoeuvre then it remains a possibility that the aircraft went into a dive and crashed straight into Lake Superior. The theory does not explain how the radar contact completely disappeared when it merged with the unidentified blip. However, to become the pilot of a high-performance (for its time) interceptor required candidates of the highest calibre and it would be expected that Moncla had passed the stringent medical for airmen.

On 16 April 1954, new information concerning the timing of a low-flying aircraft was passed to the operations officer at the headquarters of the 5th Air Rescue Group. The information was sent by R.O. Wilson, father of the Scorpion's missing radar operator, Robert Wilson. Mr Wilson had been checking out a report of a low-flying aircraft that had been heard in the vicinity of Limer, Ontario, at around the time the Scorpion had gone missing. This report was dismissed at the time of the disappearance as not being of any relevance because the time the aircraft was heard was different to when the Scorpion disappeared. Despite the time differentiation, a search had been carried out.

Limer is a small township about 12 miles (20km) from the shore of Lake Superior and it lies just over 70 miles (115km) to the east of the last known location of the Scorpion before it disappeared. The information about the timing of hearing the low-flying aircraft possibly being incorrect was eventually passed by the HQ of the 5th Air Rescue Group to the 49th Air Rescue Squadron on 6 May 1954. This was five and a half months after the disappearance of the Scorpion and three weeks after the new information had been received by the HQ. However, while it seems there was some failure to act with any urgency over the aircraft and its crew, the ground in that area was covered in snow to a depth of 2 to 4ft. So, there was little point in a fruitless search that most likely wouldn't turn up anything. Weather forecasters estimated that the snow would have mostly disappeared by 10 May and a search was scheduled to start on that date with the forward base for the operation to be located at Kinross Air Force Base.

The renewed search was carried out in co-ordination with the RCAF Search and Rescue Centre at Trenton, Ontario, which reopened the search mission to cover the Canadian side. Robert Wilson's father asked to be present at Kinross when the mission was reopened. By this stage any hope of finding his son alive must have been very slim, but at least the location of the aircraft could help to bring some closure. The weather was below minimum standards on 10 May 1954 and the new search did not get under way until 0757hrs on 13 May 1954. The search zone was split into northern and southern areas. The US crews searched the southern zone but came up with nothing. Despite the additional three days to start the search because of the weather, the northern part of the search zone to be covered by the RCAF was still covered with snow and the lakes were still covered with ice. It was to be a further five days before the snow disappeared and the ice melted so the RCAF could start searching its zone. Despite the renewed search, which was given some impetus by the report that the Scorpion may have come down in that area, nothing turned up. The operation was scaled down and closed until any new information came in as to the aircraft's whereabouts. It was a crushing blow for Mr Wilson and the relatives.

As strange as it was, aircraft disappeared and crashed regularly in this area, including USAF aircraft. Also, by an odd coincidence, the 433rd FIS had lost another Scorpion earlier that same day, although it did not disappear in the same way Moncla's and Wilson's aircraft did. This other Scorpion was flown by 1st Lt John Schmidt with radar operator Capt Glen Collins. They had taken off from their home base at Truax Field at 12.30 p.m. on a routine flight to check the afterburners on the newly installed J-35-A-47 engines. The aircraft climbed to 40,000ft (12,192m) and was transmitting data to a ground recording unit. Once the tests had been carried out, the transmissions stopped and the aircraft prepared to return to base. Twelve minutes later the Scorpion was seen in a steep dive. The aircraft started to pull out about 500ft (152m) above the ground, but it was too late and it crashed, killing both crew members. The canopy had been ejected but the crew were still in the aircraft when it hit the ground 7 miles (11.3km) south of Truax Field. The cause of the crash was not determined. Although there was nothing to directly link the loss of both aircraft from the unit, the loss and deaths of four aircrew within twelve hours of each other was a hard blow for the unit to take.

Besides the loss of military aircraft around the lake and surrounding area, there were also numerous accidents and losses of civil light aircraft. Some of these crashes took place in the sparsely populated areas around the shores of Lake Superior and the wreckage would lie undiscovered for many years. It was considered a possibility that this may have happened to the Scorpion flown by Moncla and Wilson. In 1968, a couple of prospectors found the wreckage of an aircraft in Cozens Cove, in the Alona Bay area which is 70 miles (112.7km) north of Sault Ste. Marie. It is an area covered in bush and the Algoma Forest, and the wreckage looked like it had been there for some time. The Ontario Police arrived and removed the tail section from the wreckage. An examination of the tail and other parts of the wreckage showed it to be made of heavier metal than that normally used in aircraft construction, leading them to conclude that the parts were from a jet aircraft. Naturally, the assumption was made that this may be the missing Scorpion. The suggestion was made in an article published in the local newspaper, the *Sault Daily Star*, on 30 October 1968. Gord Heath was a researcher who had investigated the story in depth and travelled to Sault Ste. Marie in 2004 to see if he could find any more of the newspaper articles. He found two further articles published shortly after the first one. One of them stated that a Maj J.H. Parker of Kincheloe Air Base (renamed from Kinross) had positively identified the stabiliser as belonging to a high-performance military jet aircraft. However, the missing F-89C was ruled out. Also dismissed was the possibility that the parts came from military aerial targets used in the area in the 1958–60 period.

Although the Scorpion and military targets were ruled out, what the article did not say was what aircraft the stabiliser was from, nor how the F-89C and aerial targets had been ruled out. There had been a number of previous disappearances and crashes of civil and military aircraft in the area in which the wreckage was discovered, and, apart from the wreckage found in 1968, only one other wreck site had been found, that of a civil light aircraft that had crashed in thick fog in 1963. Further afield in the shore area of the lake and the immediate bush and forest-covered hinterland there had been a number of disappearances of aircraft in the post-war years and up to 1969. These included an RCAF T-33 trainer that was making its way back to its base at North Bay and came down in very bad weather. The disappearance of the T-33 took place only two months after the disappearance of the Scorpion and despite the fact that it was believed the jet had come down only 30 miles (48km) or so from North Bay, no trace of the plane or pilot Charles Ness was ever found. Further south, in March 1969 another T-33, a USAF example, had crashed 18 miles south of Kincheloe with one of the two crew on board having ejected but he was never found. It was a desolate area and the fact that aircraft and aircrew had completely disappeared in the past was not a complete surprise.

In the case of Moncla's and Wilson's aircraft, the presence of Lake Superior underneath them led many to think that the Scorpion had gone into an uncontrollable dive and gone straight into the lake and disappeared. Despite the lack of debris on the surface, it was certainly plausible. However, there were also a number of people who were disturbed by the circumstances. The unexplained radar blip and the merging of the Scorpion with this and its immediate disappearance after merging led them to think that whatever the blip was, it had somehow caused the disappearance.

The case would have probably faded into history, to be brought up occasionally in discussions of missing aircraft cases. However, the mystery of the disappearance of the

Scorpion was given a major boost a couple of years later when a man named Donald E. Keyhoe became involved. There had already been speculation that the strange nature of the Scorpion's total disappearance without any trace was due to a hostile alien craft. This was a contentious area, with UFO theorists being dismissed as cranks and screwballs by many, including USAF Col Watson, who was in charge of the Air Technical Intelligence Centre in Dayton, Ohio. Col Watson's opinion was that these people were either 'crackpots, idiots or religious fanatics'. However, Keyhoe was not some spotty juvenile reading UFO comics in the basement of his parents' house. He was a qualified pilot and had served in the United States Marine Air Corps (USMAC). He also had the support of many businessmen, scientists and military personnel as well as both military and civil pilots.

Despite Keyhoe's respectable credentials, he could be, and was, dismissed by some as just another UFO conspiracy theorist. However, it is useful to remember the context of the time. In the early to mid 1950s the USA was in the grip of Cold War paranoia and the idea that Earth could be invaded by alien forces from outer space at any time had a large and receptive audience. Keyhoe's position on the whole issue of UFO sightings and the official response to them was shown in a celebrated TV interview with journalist and presenter Mike Wallace on 3 August 1958, almost five years after the disappearance of the Scorpion over Lake Superior. Wallace conducted prime time TV thirty-minute interviews with celebrities and figures of public interest from 1957 to 1960. Keyhoe was brought on to the show and introduced as the director of a private group known as the National Investigations Committee on Aerial Phenomena and he was also acknowledged as a former Marine Air Corps major. Unlike a run-of-the-mill TV interview, Wallace had prepared extensively for the show and had contacted the US Air Force to ask for its views beforehand. Specifically, Wallace was in touch with the Air Technical Intelligence Centre at the Pentagon.

The premise of the whole interview was to discuss evidence of flying saucers from other worlds visiting Earth and that this was being officially covered up by both the US Air Force and the government itself. The interview took place with the background of the Air Force Project Blue Book in people's minds. Blue Book was started in 1952 and was the third study (the other two were Project Sign and Project Grudge) to determine if UFOs were a threat and to scientifically analyse data collected from UFO sightings.

As to why the government and US Air Force should bother to cover up visits by aliens, Keyhoe pointed out the hysteria caused by the Orson Welles' radio broadcast of *War of the Worlds* for Halloween in 1938. Although the extent of the supposed mass panic over the broadcast was proved to be a myth, there were enough people who were disturbed and frightened by the broadcast and thought it was real. Many people at the time thought that the USA was being invaded by aliens who were advancing on New York and that Welles was giving a factual account of the invasion. Keyhoe told Wallace that the government did not want any kind of a repeat of these scenes, all the more so if there was any potential truth in the sightings of UFOs. There was no dispute between the US Air Force and government on the one side and UFO investigators such as Keyhoe on the other that there were unknown lights and objects appearing in the skies. Where the clash came was in the interpretation of what they might be.

Wallace pointed out that Richard Horner, Assistant Secretary of the Air Force for Research and Development, had said that all but a small percentage of unidentified flying objects had been definitely attributed to natural phenomena that were neither mysterious nor dire. Wallace said this included weather balloons, mirages and ordinary sky phenomena such as meteorites and even other aircraft.

Keyhoe's response to this was that the Air Force was deliberately misleading the public about the sightings. He did not dispute that many sightings were down to weather phenomena, balloons and other aircraft but his view was that there was a small percentage of completely unexplained sightings that were being covered up. Furthermore, Keyhoe said that a number of sightings had been made by high-ranking Air Force pilots and many airline captains who were qualified and well versed in aviation matters. They were also used to seeing aerial phenomena, and their word could not be quite so easily dismissed. Keyhoe said that standard Air Force policy was to deny any UFO or alien involvement in these sightings and personnel just had to go along with it, whatever they may have felt privately.

Keyhoe mentioned a figure of 800 witnesses on a list he kept and this included some big names in aviation, right up to the rank of a colonel in the Air Force. Keyhoe asked that if these men were all screwballs and cranks then why were they still on the job flying in the Air Force and the civilian ones carrying passengers? He also said that the list included radar operators who had seen UFOs on their screens.

Wallace changed tack and asked Keyhoe where he thought the flying saucers were coming from? Keyhoe replied that he didn't know but said that there was a possibility Mars was being used as a base. He didn't think they originated from Mars but pointed out that whenever Mars had approached Earth in the previous ten years there had been an increase in sightings of UFOs and that this had been acknowledged officially. Keyhoe pointed out that the Canadians had set up an official project named Project Magnet with an observatory at Shirleys Bay on the Ottawa River, near Ottawa, to track aerial phenomena related to the Mars approaches. In its one year of operation this observatory had made one sighting on a gravimeter (an instrument used to measure the difference in the force of gravity from one place to another) of a very large object, but the project was closed down due to the expenditure. Wallace pointed out to Keyhoe that surely the project would not have been closed down if it had made such a sighting or if it was believed this phenomena existed, to which Keyhoe's response was that many of the people who had worked on the project continued to carry out research in their own time and expense.

Wallace then asked what he thought such aliens would look like. Keyhoe said that it was just speculation as to their appearance and intelligence but scientists believed (mentioning Dr Howard Shafly in particular) that out of the estimated one hundred million planets in the universe that might be inhabited and that if evolution had begun in some of them at the same time as Earth, then it could be expected that similar types of beings to humans could have evolved in intelligence and appearance. It was at this point in the interview that the disappearance of Moncla and Wilson in the Scorpion over Lake Superior came up. Wallace asked him what might these aliens want or be looking for? Keyhoe replied that he did not feel that there was hostile intent from them. He said that there had been what he felt were merely accidents involving alien craft and aircraft. He described a pilot who had been killed in his aircraft in 1948 when he was chasing a UFO and then crashed. He then described the loss of the Scorpion with both pilots over Lake Superior and that this too had been an accident with no hostile intent. It was during this period in the early 1950s Keyhoe said that there was a great deal more openness and cooperation from the Air Force about what might have been going on.

Both Keyhoe and Wallace discussed the issues and difficulties of communication with aliens but Keyhoe's view was that these sightings of UFOs were long-range surveys on the part of the UFOs and their purpose was to do no more than observe. There had never been any verified claim of an attempt at communication, although there had been individuals who had claimed to communicate with aliens. These, however, tended to be taken with a pinch of salt.

Keyhoe spoke of a policy of cooperation and friendship with complete openness on these matters up until

1952–53. This was when the Scorpion had disappeared but Keyhoe did not say whether this incident had affected the open policy of the Air Force, although there was no doubt there had been a hardening of attitudes on transparency after the loss. He also pointed out that in 1947 the Air Technical Intelligence Centre at Dayton sent secret documents to the Commanding General of the Air Force stating that they believed the UFOs to be real. In the following year the Dayton Air Technical Intelligence Centre sent secret documents to the Air Force Commanding General, Hoyt Vandenburg, which stated that they believed a small percentage of the unexplained phenomena were interplanetary spaceships. In 1952, Keyhoe explained that analysis had been carried out on radar images of the extreme manoeuvres of these unidentified objects, and in the following year, the CIA and the Air Force convened a panel that met at the Pentagon and concluded that whilst definitive proof was still lacking of spaceships or flying saucers, they accepted there was a strong circumstantial case for their existence. Keyhoe and Wallace then discussed a claim that Keyhoe had made on a number of occasions with regard to four documents held by the Air Force that contained important and secret information on the UFOs. Wallace had been told by the Pentagon that three of the four documents simply did not exist but that he was welcome to see the fourth document. Wallace quoted a line from the fourth document that said the Pentagon panel recommended that the national security agencies take immediate steps to strip UFOs of the special status they had been given with the resultant aura of mystery they had unfortunately acquired. It went on to further suggest that an integrated programme be designed to reassure the public by showing the total lack of evidence of the forces behind the phenomena.

Despite this attempt at reassurance by the government and regardless of the issue of the missing three documents they said did not exist, Keyhoe pointed out to Wallace that he had spoken to hundreds of pilots, radar operators and guided missile trackers who had seen these UFOs and that the government number of sightings that could not be accounted for was 1.9 per cent of the total. He also pointed out that the government had not brought a halt to its investigations and that it was still investigating what was going on ('current' was the word used). Keyhoe referred to Special Report 14, which he said was the 'Bible' for these matters and said he had a copy of it. In the back of it there was a table showing 3,201 cases that the government had examined, which showed the breakdown of all the cases including the unsolved ones. Since this report had been produced there had been further cases. There was a category that remained unsolved due to 'insufficient information', which was 12 per cent. This Special Report 14 was an official bulletin released by the Department of Defense and covered the period from June 1955 to June 1957.

Wallace's response was that the department had been quite open with him and willingly showed him what it had in order to prepare for his interview with Keyhoe. Wallace went so far as to use the word 'hoax', which Keyhoe took exception to, at which Wallace apologised and changed his wording to 'misinformation'. However, he maintained the theme of questioning the

whole idea of UFOs and mentioned an astrophysi-
cist, Dr Donald Menzel, a Harvard professor who was
critical of UFO sightings. He described the sightings
as being similar to 'the wrapper of somebody's lunch
moving around on the air'.

Wallace once again came back to his theme of why
would the government hide these sightings? Keyhoe
started by saying he did not agree with Menzel and that
he knew many people equally as well qualified as the
professor who took the opposing view on UFO sightings. He followed this by stating the government treated
the public like children and pointed out that the government had kept the H-bomb hidden from the public and
had also hidden the fact that submarine-launched missiles could hit the USA from the Gulf of Mexico and
both east and west coastlines very easily. He wasn't blam-
ing the US Air Force in general, just a small group who
were keeping information under wraps.

He then referred to a show that he was to take part in,
but part of what he was going to refer to was deleted from
the programme on the instruction of Air Force chiefs.
In fact, the deleted items had been included in a book
written by Captain Edward Ruppelt and referred to the
secrecy concerning the Air Force investigations of UFOs.
Ruppelt had been an advisor to President Truman and
Keyhoe said that although he had been intimidated into
leaving out parts of what he wanted to discuss, Ruppelt
had faced no censure nor even the threat of court martial
for writing about the same thing.

The interview moved onto Wallace asking about three
new reports that Keyhoe had obtained that were said to

prove beyond a doubt that flying saucers existed. Keyhoe said that it should convince a lot of people because of the names involved, many of whom were 'high up' including a top scientist who he said was known to 'everybody'. However, Keyhoe was unwilling to name some of the individuals at their own request because they feared official 'ridicule'. The exasperated interviewer asked Keyhoe why someone should fear official ridicule over alerting the country to what was a serious national security issue. He replied that he was merely acting as he had been asked to and referred to an incident in 1951 when a UFO circled a US fleet in Korean waters for half an hour. The radar was tracking the UFO and several aircraft were launched to intercept it, but it then left the area at more than 1,000mph. The person who had provided Keyhoe with this information asked that he not be identified.

He then referred to another report on the sighting of UFOs in California on 11 November 1957 by four missile designers and engineers. They had observed an elliptical-shaped object and two small round disc-shaped objects on a clear cloudless day and they believed the speeds of the objects to be above 5,000mph. Keyhoe pointed out to Wallace that despite the official Air Force policy of not having anything to conceal, as stated by Richard Horner, Assistant Secretary of the Air Force for Research and Development, an attempt for a UFO advert to be placed in an Air Force magazine was stopped as it was contrary to US Air Force policy. Captain Gregory Oldenburg, a public information officer at Langley Air Base, had intervened and stopped an advert in the base newspaper that was asking if anyone interested in UFOs would like to form a small group. Oldenburg gave the reason that dissemination of information on UFOs was contrary to Air Force policy and against regulations.

They went on to discuss the reports of two men who had claimed to have spoken to aliens from Venus. Keyhoe said he didn't believe them but would be willing to consider their claims if they provided more evidence and were willing to undergo lie-detector tests. The interview finished with Wallace asking Keyhoe what he would like to see done about flying saucers that was not currently being done. He replied that he would like to see people writing to their Congressmen to insist on open hearings by the Senate Committee. Wallace's response to this was that the Air Force had already spoken with members of the Senate Sub-Committee and they had not expressed any interest in holding hearings on this issue.

Keyhoe was asked if he had seen an actual flying saucer, to which he replied that he had not but had spoken to hundreds of credible witnesses who had. The interview ended with a conclusion by Wallace that holds as true in the first half of the twenty-first century as it did in 1958: that the flying-saucer controversy was deadlocked in contradictory statements and interpretation of facts.

In 2005 the story of the missing Scorpion and its crew returned to the public spotlight when it was claimed that the wreckage of the aircraft had been found on the bottom of Lake Superior. A company called the Great Lakes Dive Company had reportedly located the wreckage of the fighter at a depth of 200ft (61m). The company supposedly specialised in shipwrecks that contained valuable cargo and claimed to have investors who had funded this particular expedition, which was to find the luxury yacht *Gunilda*. The *Gunilda* was built in Leith, Scotland, in 1897 and owned by William L. Harkness, an American businessman who had inherited a large share of Standard Oil from his father. On 11 August 1911, Harkness was sailing across Lake Superior with some similarly well-heeled friends when the yacht hit some rocks at McGarvey Shoal, near Rossport, Ontario. Rossport was well over 100 miles (160.93km) away from the last recorded point of the Scorpion. The passengers were taken off the vessel fairly quickly and it sank with their belongings still in their cabins.

The dive company had trouble with its sonar equipment and by the time it was working, it was too late in the year to continue the search for the *Gunilda*. The divers made the decision to search for the missing Scorpion instead. Quite why it was too late in the year to work on the *Gunilda* but not to search for the Scorpion in the same lake was not explained. In any event, the company announced it had found the Scorpion on the lake bed and said it was confirmed as the missing aircraft because of its raised tail.

The following summer, the company returned to the spot with side-scanner sonar and announced that the aircraft's canopy was still intact, so the remains of Moncla and Wilson were presumed to be still in the aircraft. Further examination showed that one wing had been sheared off. The divers identified the aircraft from the serial 51-5853 on the tail. To add to the excitement of the find, the side-scanner radar also picked up another half-buried object which appeared to be metallic with a bulge that was taken by 'ufologists' to be the bulge seen in the centre of flying saucers. This metallic object lay on the bed of the lake about 200ft (61m) away from the Scorpion. Enhanced imaging found the bulge to be around 8ft by 15ft and similar to the Scorpion's nacelle. It all seemed too good to be true and that is where the problems began.

The dive company spokesman was an Adam Jimenez and after he had described the find he said that the company could not resume its examination of the wreckage because the Canadian authorities would not allow the company to go back to the *Gunilda* site if it did not inform them of the exact location of the aircraft, which they believed had sunk on the Canadian side of the lake. This (supposedly) put the company in an awkward position as it needed to dive on the *Gunilda* to keep its investors happy, but equally it did not want to release the location for the missing plane in case it was beaten to a full examination of the wreckage by another party. In addition, the company had been searching for two sunken French minesweepers, the *Inkermann* and the *Cerisoles*, which had vanished without trace on Lake Superior in November 1918. Whilst it could be understood that the company found itself in an awkward position, there were many sceptics of the claims, not least some within the UFO community.

The Mutual UFO Network Inc. (MUFON) is one of the principal organisations devoted to UFO investigations and it looked into the claims made by the dive company, beginning with the company itself. With each stage of the investigation, anomalies were thrown up. The company claimed to be based in Michigan, but the Michigan Division of Corporations had no record of a business with this name. When asked about this discrepancy, Jimenez said the company was in the process of moving from being incorporated to limited liability. Earlier, Jimenez had contradicted his explanation by stating that it was already a limited liability company. And so, the contradictions and evasions piled up.

The Great Lakes company was unable to give any details of who its backers were or the equipment it used, the reason given being that it was being 'threatened'. Who exactly was behind the threats was unclear and Jimenez said the company was forced to change its phone numbers and become anonymous. Jimenez had also claimed that a number of restrictions in connection with its examination of the Scorpion had been placed on it by the Ontario Ministry of Culture. Enquiries showed that this information was not correct. That left the side scans of the aircraft and the metallic object on the lake bed. Two experts examined them closely, with one concluding that the scans were definitely fabricated and the other stating that whilst it was possible they were genuine, there was some doubt about their authenticity.

Despite the detractors, there were some who wanted to believe the Scorpion had been found and accepted the various explanations given by Jimenez. He didn't help himself by his claim in an interview that he had graduated with a degree in computer engineering from Kettering University in Michigan. Enquiries showed that Kettering had never had anyone of his name enrolled with them. The story of the Great Lakes Dive Company's discovery of the Scorpion and a possible UFO petered out in 2006. The company and Jimenez were never heard from again. Many people believed that apart from being a hoax, the whole thing had been organised in order to profit financially from a website it had set up by attracting as many visitors to it as possible.

One peculiar aspect of the whole case is the seeming lack of input from the Canadian military. Of course, the Canadians did all they could to help in the search, but there seems to have been little interest from that side in investigating the strange disappearance of a US military aircraft within their jurisdiction.

There are numerous versions of the Kinross Incident on the internet and one or two versions have given incorrect information regarding the flight path of the unidentified radar blip/RCAF C-47. These accounts state that the intruder, or unidentified radar contact, is first identified flying over the restricted airspace of the Soo Locks, which are just to the north of Kinross Air Force Base and almost 200 miles (322km) to the east of the Pillow radar station at Calumet on the Keweenaw Peninsula. It is then tracked and the F-89C is vectored on to the radar contact, which is supposedly flying west, and the two 'blips' merge at a point over Lake Superior almost 200 miles (322km) west of the Soo Locks and to the north of the Pillow station. The problem with this narrative is that the RCAF C-47 was flying from west to east, from Winnipeg to Sudbury, not the other way round. If the C-47 had been over the Soo Locks when it was first picked up by Naples radar it would have been east of the Locks in the time taken for the F-89C to make the interception. In other words, the C-47 would have been well to the east, not to the west, and would have been starting its approach to Sudbury and descending to land there. Gord Heath, who began investigating this story in 2001, had managed to track down Gerald Fosberg, the commander of the RCAF C-47, who confirmed his route as heading east from Winnipeg to Sudbury.

Furthermore, as the C-47 was travelling from west to east, and even allowing for it being 30 miles (48km) off course (which Fosberg says he wasn't), when Naples radar station made the first contact, the C-47 could not have been over the Soo Locks. It would have been coming out from land onto Lake Superior at the far western end, far away from the Soo Locks at the time of the first contact. This is assuming a cruising speed of around 155mph (250kmph) at 7,000ft. If this is correct then Naples could not have identified the C-47 as the intruder.

There are a few scenarios to explain what may have happened. The first two possibilities involve a violent manoeuvre by the Scorpion. The first, as previously mentioned, concerns the RCAF C-47. Ignoring the issue that Fosberg says he was nowhere near the interception point, if the C-47 had been the aircraft that the Scorpion came upon, Moncla was at the same height and closing rapidly. It is more than possible he came upon the C-47 at an angle that would have forced him to make a sudden and violent turn to avoid the other aircraft. When the two radar blips merged, the Scorpion disappeared at that moment and the C-47 carried on its track. Fosberg says neither he nor his crew saw or heard anything, notwithstanding that he claims he was 30 miles north of that position anyway. Even if Fosberg had been off course without realising it, and he had seen another aircraft pass very close to him, he would quite likely have radioed to report a 'near miss' and also would have had to file a 'near miss' report on landing at Sudbury.

The effect of such a violent and sudden manoeuvre could well have forced the Scorpion into an uncontrollable dive that Moncla could not have pulled out of, and ended up being destroyed on impact with the lake surface.

There was speculation regarding the lack of Canadian (RCAF) input to the presence of an unidentified aircraft either in their airspace or very close to it. That can be put down to the fact the RCAF knew one of its aircraft was travelling from Winnipeg to Sudbury. Another question is if the RCAF was aware of an unidentified aircraft in that location and had not tied it up with Fosberg's C-47 then why did it not launch an RCAF interceptor from the main base at RCAF North Bay to investigate? RCAF North Bay, which lay to the north of Lake Superior, was built in 1951 and its sole purpose was air defence, to monitor and protect the skies. At first this was limited to around North Bay, then it was expanded to the Northern Ontario area of Canada, then east, central and Arctic Canada, before eventually covering all of Canada. This was an area equivalent to the size of Europe. However, at the time of the disappearance of Moncla and Wilson's aircraft, RCAF North Bay had no interceptors based there because it was in the middle of having one unit, 445 Squadron, depart on 31 August 1953 and was awaiting the arrival of the next one, 419 Squadron, which did not arrive there until 15 March 1954.

The Kinross Incident

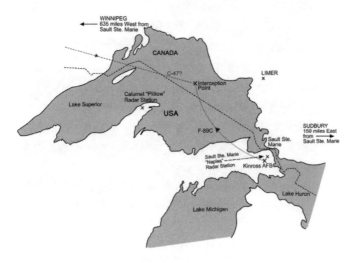

Map of Lake Superior showing the interception on 23 November 1953 by F-89C Scorpion 51-5853 with relevant locations. (*bhardwaz – FIVERR*)

An F-89C taking off from Eglin AFB, Florida. (*Courtesy of the National Museum of the United States Air Force*)

USAF Lieutenants Weld and Benfermum scramble to their F-89C at Kinross AFB. (*Courtesy of the National Museum of the United States Air Force*)

RCAF C-47 VC-912 – This is the actual aircraft that Moncla's and Wilson's F-89C was supposedly intercepting on the night of 23 November 1953. This C-47 also met a tragic end twenty-four years later. (*Courtesy Larry Milberry*)

One theory that has been put forward for the radar blip for the RCAF C-47 is that it was actually a phantom radar echo, not the RCAF C-47, which was further north, as confirmed by the pilot Gerry Fosberg. If this was a phantom radar echo, it seems odd that the Scorpion disappeared when it merged with it because there should have been nothing there. One explanation is that there may have been clouds or smaller formations of industrial-type chaff. In the early 1950s there was not as much concern for the environment as there would be in later years. At the time, there was considerable mining and industrial production over a wide area near Lake Superior. Zinc was smelted and there was mining of cadmium, silver and lead on the Canadian side. On the US side, iron ore (taconite) was mined as well as copper. New arrivals to the Pillow (Calumet) radar station were told they were in Copper Country. There were also coal mining, steel foundries and steel fabrication plants. Port Arthur in Ontario had the world's largest grain elevators and nearby in Fort William was the world's largest malt plant. It is quite possible that clouds of this industrial 'waste' would be present in the atmosphere over Lake Superior. The argument against the chaff is that the unidentified 'blip' had been observed travelling at a height of 7,000ft (2,134m), although the radar echo may have been confused by a large cloud of industrial waste spread out over a wide area.

Following on from a near miss with the RCAF C-47, there was other aerial activity in this area at the time that was not particularly well regulated. There was a small airport named Isle Royale Sands at Houghton, which was

20 miles (32km) south of the Pillow (Calumet) radar station. Isle Royale Sands Airport received three to four mail flights a week as well as passenger flights by the small regional airline North Central Airlines. The mail was carried in old Beech 18s and Cessna Bobcats. There were other regular visitors to this airport in the form of Second World War surplus trainers and utility and communications aircraft such as Avro Ansons and Airspeed Oxfords. Thunder Bay in Ontario (actually two separate places in those days; Fort William and Port Arthur) was approximately 50 miles (80.46km) to the north-west and also saw regular flights by mail aircraft and various training and utility aircraft. Added to this mix were other light aircraft used for sports events and by hunters and fishermen, which together made the situation ripe for potential confusion.

Flight plans were supposed to be filed but not everyone did and although the mail planes flew to schedules and filed flight plans, due to the frequent appalling winter weather in Lake Superior these old mail planes regularly flew off course and showed up on radar as intercept bogeys. Radio communication between the civil authorities and Air Force Ground Observer Corps and the radar and interceptor system was haphazard in such a large unpopulated area and the small airport at Houghton was the only airfield of note in the area; even that did not have an operational control tower until the 1960s.

What was unique about the Kinross Incident with regards to possible alien involvement was that the crew had completely disappeared along with their aircraft. This was the only known case up to this time and it caught people's imagination because there was an underlying assumption that 'alien technology', assuming it existed, was always vastly superior to anything produced by humans on Earth. There was no evidence with which to back this up but it was, and still is, generally held to be true. The UFO theorists only had to point to the fact that Moncla and Wilson were there one minute with a large, modern interceptor and had completely disappeared the next minute. There are many accounts of UFOs travelling at speeds of several thousand miles an hour and changing direction at these speeds at physically impossible angles. Taking these observations into account, the argument against a UFO is that it would seem odd that it would mimic a slow-moving aircraft travelling across Lake Superior at a very low airspeed at a height of only 7,000ft (2,134m).

Whether or not one believes in the UFO theory or whether it was just a straightforward accident, the element of bad luck certainly rubbed off on the RCAF C-47 flown by Gerry Fosberg that night. After its career with the RCAF, it was sold by the Crown Assets Disposal Corporation in December 1971 and given a civil registration, CF-BKV. It flew with a number of civil operators and ended up with Patricia Air Services. On 12 May 1977, it was taking off from Pickle Lake, Ontario, when an engine caught fire. The landing gear would not retract, which resulted in the aircraft nosing over and coming to rest inverted on the surface of the lake, before it sank. One of the two pilots on board was killed in the accident.

CHAPTER 4

A SRI LANKAN MYSTERY

Philip Upali Wijewardene was a man who, on the face of it, had it all. The 44-year-old Sri Lankan possessed film-star looks and was a wealthy man. Estimates of his wealth vary, with some putting it at $300 million and others placing it as high as $3.2 billion in 1983. He had been educated at Royal College Colombo and Queens' College, Cambridge. Wijewardene was also well connected and was a cousin of the Sri Lankan President, J.R. Jayewardene. Before becoming chairman of the Upali Group, he had begun his career as a management trainee with Lever Brothers in Ceylon and had struck out on his own following a disagreement. After leaving Lever Brothers, his uncle had given him shares in his Ceylon Chocolates Company. Whilst it can be said that Wijewardene was given a good start in his business life with his wealthy background and connections, he was also a shrewd and talented man. One other factor that made Wijewardene stand out from many businessmen of all nationalities was his personal kindness towards people who worked for and came into contact with him. For instance, each time he left his Malaysian residence Cocoa Hill after a stay, he would personally give each member of the domestic staff there $100 as a gift, over and above their salaries.

Using the Lever Brothers business model, he formed the Upali group of companies and built up a diverse range of companies that encompassed electronics, car manufacturing (assembling Mazda and Fiat cars), aviation, horse racing, publishing and print media, as well as branded consumer goods.

The Upali Group had substantial interests in the Far East and it was for this reason that on 13 February 1983, Wijewardene found himself in Malaysia. On that day, he was winding up his stay at Cocoa Hill, the large residence that he had built at No. 104 Jalang Punkit Pantai, Kuala Lumpur. He had arrived there two weeks previously, on 31 January 1983 and involved himself with his business affairs.

The complexity of his business affairs in Malaysia were a miniature version of the wider Upali Group. In 1969 he had acquired two Malaysian businesses; the Perak River Coconut Company Ltd (which he changed to Upali Investments Holdings Ltd) and the Lower Perak Company Ltd (which he changed to Upali Enterprises Ltd). A few years later, he began the manufacture of chocolates in Malaysia through another company named Upali (Malaysia) Sdn Bhd, which ran the Kandos Chocolates factory. The Malaysian companies were owned in turn by a Hong Kong company named Kuril Enterprises Ltd. Kuril Enterprises was itself at the centre of a web of Far Eastern companies as well as several in Hong Kong. The Hong Kong companies were linked to a trust, which was linked to a company in London (Grand Central Investment Holdings Plc). This was further linked to a company in Liechtenstein (Kuril Anstalt).

Despite the fact that the plantations covered thousands of acres and there was plenty to do, Wijewardene's driver, named Selladurai, who lived at Cocoa Hill and had worked for Upali (Malaysia) Sdn Bhd for seven years, later stated to investigators that in the two weeks since his arrival in Kuala Lumpur on 31 January to his departure for the airport, Wijewardene did not once set foot outside the residence. Selladurai lived in the main house and was very attentive to 'the chairman', as he called Wijewardene.

He (Selladurai) said that the chairman must have had a lot on his mind as he had noted that the second last night before his return to Sri Lanka he had been up all night until 7 a.m. the following day (12 February 1983) and saw that Wijewardene had smoked no fewer than eighty cigarettes. On his last night at Cocoa Hill, Selladurai noted that the chairman did not retire to bed until 3.30 a.m. on the morning of the day he was due to leave to return to Sri Lanka. Although the chairman had said nothing about what may have been bothering him at this time, there were two possibilities put forward by those who knew him. The first concerned horse racing. Wijewardene was very keen on racing and his horse had just lost a race, which annoyed and upset him greatly because he was convinced it had stood a good chance of winning. The other factor that may have affected his behaviour was also mentioned by Selladurai. He was to later state that Wijewardene's 'Man Friday', 35-year-old Athula Senanayake, had told him he noticed that the chairman had not phoned Colombo at all during the first week of his stay at Cocoa Hill. Senanayake had laughed and said it was because he had had a quarrel with his wife before he left.

The day before Wijewardene and his party were due to depart Kuala Lumpur for Sri Lanka, the Upali Group executive jet arrived at Subang Airport, Kuala Lumpur, bringing two people from Singapore. These two were to travel to Colombo with Wijewardene. They were the Upali director, 30-year-old Ananda Pelimuhandiram, and a newspaper reporter, Migara Ratnatunge. After disembarking, both men made their way to Cocoa Hill in Pelimuhandiram's chauffeur-driven car.

On the morning of 13 February 1983 and prior to leaving for the airport, Wijewardene followed an established routine. He arose at 11 a.m. and began preparing to leave. At midday, he had instructed his driver Govinda Raju to pick up the two pilots of the Upali Company Learjet from the Suban View Hotel, where they were staying, and to take them to Subang. Raju had been with the company for two years and, like Selladurai, he was one of the chairman's band of loyal retainers who lived at Cocoa Hill.

Three other people were present at Cocoa Hill who were to accompany Wijewardene on the flight back to Colombo. They were his 'Man Friday' Senanayake, Ananda Pelimuhandiram and Sithapalam Muruga Ratnam. Although Wijewardene had two drivers to chauffeur him around, Senanyake also drove for him and most of the time acted as his personal chauffeur. This duty was in addition to his role as a kind of butler to the chairman. Senanayake went everywhere with him. He was married with two children, but his life was closely linked to the chairman's busy schedule and he also acted as the steward on board the Upali Learjet.

Ananda Pelimuhandiram was from Gampaha, a city to the north-east of Colombo, and was unmarried. He had joined the company as a management trainee and risen quickly through the ranks to become a director by the age of 30. Ratnam, the third man, was the company lawyer and had known the chairman for many years, since the start of Wijewardene's overseas business ventures in the Far East, Europe and the USA. In addition, Ratnam was also the chairman of Kuril Enterprises in Hong Kong. On paper, this gave him a leading role in the labyrinth of Upali companies as Kuril Enterprises in Hong Kong was central to the financial running of them. Furthermore, Ratnam was the chairman of Kuril Enterprises while Wijewardene was only a director of the Hong Kong Company. With his financial and legal expertise, plus his long association with the overseas companies, Ratnam was crucial to the whole operation.

Selladurai and Senanayake had both packed the chairman's clothes and Theresa the cook had made sandwiches for the flight. These were packed into a container with biscuits and a plastic bag containing ice cubes. Senanayake had packed a dozen cans of Coca-Cola along with two dozen candle-type bulbs and a bottle of Coffee Mate. The amount of baggage amongst them for the relatively small aircraft amounted to travelling bags for Wijewardene, Senanayake and Ratnam with Ratnam and Wijewardene both carrying briefcases as well. Three cars left for the airport. Selladurai took Wijewardene, Senanayake and Ratnam in one car, with the driver Raju taking all the bags and food in a second car. The third car, which belonged to the Upali Malaysia technical director Susantha Gunawardene, contained Upali director Ananda Pelimuhandiram. Selladurai was an observant man and he later recalled that there appeared to be nothing untoward in the behaviour of the whole party prior to their leaving Cocoa Hill. This is notwithstanding his comments regarding the quiet and pensive mood of Wijewardene over the previous two nights.

The group's departure to Colombo was originally scheduled for 1600hrs. Both the Learjet pilots had arrived some considerable time ahead of the group. The aircraft commander was Captain Noel Anandappa and the co-pilot was Sydney de Zoysa, both Sri Lankans. A flight plan had been lodged with the Colombo Air Traffic Control Centre with the Learjet using the R61 air corridor between Kuala Lumpur and Colombo and flying at a height of 39,000ft (11,887m) at a speed of 439 nautical miles per hour. A message was sent to Colombo stating that the departure time had been put back to 1800hrs.

The three cars arrived at the airport and the party went to clear immigration and customs. After finishing the formalities, they came out and started to board the aircraft. Whether Wijewardene may have had some kind of premonition or not, he was aware that the aircraft had just been in Singapore undergoing some minor repairs. He asked de Zoysa if the repairs to the aircraft had all been carried out satisfactorily. De Zoysa replied that everything had been done. The luggage was loaded and the two pilots went on board first, followed by the rest of the party. Wijewardene, with his customary manners and attention to his staff, had gone to the two drivers (Selladurai and Raju) and the Upali Malaysia Technical Director (Gunawardene), who were all standing on the apron near the aircraft, and shaken each of their hands, thanking them before boarding the aircraft last.

The seating arrangement in the aircraft was Wijewardene in the rear seat on the left-hand side, Ratnam was seated to his right in the rear seat on the right-hand side, Pelimuhandiram was seated facing towards Ratnam and Senanayake was seated opposite to him and facing the cockpit. The door was then closed.

At this point the delayed departure time of 1800hrs had gone back even further and it was 2019hrs when the Learjet eventually contacted Kuala Lumpur air traffic control for permission to start up the engines for departure to Colombo. Once the engines were started, the ever-observant Selladurai watched nearby and noticed that both pilots spent some time looking at the instrument panel. Selladurai later stated that he felt this delay and the actions of the pilots was unusual and it was fifteen minutes before the Learjet moved and began taxiing to the runway for take-off. In light of what was to happen, Selladurai stated later that he felt something was wrong as he observed both pilots looking at the instrument panel.

At 2029hrs the aircraft requested permission from the control tower to taxi to the runway for take-off. Permission was granted and the Learjet taxied to the end of runway 33. The earlier delay in taxiing caused by the pilots checking their instruments meant that they were later leaving than intended. The aircraft reached the holding point for runway 33 at 2036hrs and informed the control tower that they were holding. Two minutes later, at 2038hrs, the aircraft was instructed to line up on the runway for take-off. They turned onto the runway and confirmed they were standing by to take-off when the tower asked them to hold briefly and to standby, which they confirmed. At 2039hrs the tower gave clearance for take-off and at 2041hrs the Learjet began its take-off roll down Subang Airport's 12,402ft (3,780m) runway, the longest in South-East Asia when it was constructed in 1965, and climbed into the night sky, heading north and preparing to make a left turn onto a westerly heading to set course for Colombo.

At 2042hrs, the crew contacted the Kuala Lumpur tower to inform it that they were passing 4,500ft (1,371m) altitude. The tower cleared the crew to make a left turn to Puger point on airway R61 and to confirm back to the tower when they had reached 8,000ft (2,438m). The crew confirmed the instruction that they would report back when they were passing through 8,000ft, which they then did. Immediately after this message, at 2043hrs, the tower instructed the crew to contact the tower on a different frequency, 132.8. The crew contacted the tower (Sector 1) on this frequency a minute later and were instructed to report when they had reached their cruising altitude of 39,000ft (11,887m). At 2044hrs, the crew reported they were climbing from 12,500ft (3,810m) to 39,000ft (11,887m) and estimated that they would reach Puger point at 2055hrs. At 2045hrs, the crew radioed again to say they would inform the tower when they had reached 39,000ft (11,887m). At 2052hrs Sector 1 had requested the aircraft to confirm their present level. The crew responded by radioing they were at 24,500ft (7,467m). At 2055hrs, the aircraft informed Kuala Lumpur control that they were passing Puger point and were climbing to 27,000ft (8,229m) on their way to 39,000ft (11,887m).

From the time that the Learjet had left the runway at Kuala Lumpur Airport to the crew informing Sector 1 that they were at 24,000ft (7,315m), fourteen minutes had elapsed. The final exchange of messages now took place. At 20.55hrs Sector 1 had instructed the Learjet crew to confirm when they were passing Medan. The crew confirmed that they would contact again when they reached Medan. This was the final message received from the Learjet.

About a quarter of an hour later, having heard nothing, Sector 1 sent a message to the Learjet at 2113hrs asking if they had reached Medan yet. With no response at 2114hrs, the tower contacted the crew of an airliner that was in the air and not far from the Learjet's last known position and asked if they could try and contact the Learjet. This aircraft was Flight Number YU601, A JAT (Yugoslav Airlines) DC-10 flying between Belgrade and Melbourne via Singapore. The DC-10 crew radioed the Learjet at 2115hrs but did not receive any response and informed Sector 1. Sector 1 replied to the Yugoslav aircraft at 2116hrs and stated that the Learjet should have crossed Medan three minutes previously and that it had not reported to them that it had done so. Sector 1 then tried to contact the Learjet and asked the crew to send a blind transmission on a high frequency, but there was no answer from the aircraft. The Upali Learjet had disappeared.

To start with, there was some confusion. There appeared to be a misunderstanding in that the crew of the Yugoslav airliner stated they had overheard the Learjet attempting to make contact with the Colombo Air Traffic Control Centre. When the transcripts of all messages from air-to-air and air-to-ground within the Colombo region were checked, this was found to be incorrect. However, the misleading information had caused the initial search to start along the eastern coast of Sri Lankan territorial waters. Once the Colombo Region transcripts were checked, the search along the eastern Sri Lankan coast was immediately called off.

The former RAF Butterworth Air Force Base at Penang was run by the Royal Australian Air Force (RAAF) at the time. The military radar facility at Penang had tracked the Learjet for seven minutes after it had passed Puger. In that time it was calculated that the aircraft had been travelling at 7.7 nautical miles per minute between 2055hrs and 2058hrs. At 2058hrs the aircraft dramatically almost doubled its speed to 14 nautical miles per minute (840 nautical miles per hour), which was faster than the speed of sound, before the aircraft disappeared from the radar screen.

In Malaysia and Indonesia, a search and rescue operation got under way. At 3.30 a.m. on the morning of 14 February 1983, six and a half hours after the disappearance of the Learjet, the Sri Lankan High Commissioner for Malaysia was informed that the Upali aircraft had not reached Colombo and was overdue. The authorities in

Sri Lanka asked the High Commissioner to immediately contact the Indonesian authorities and ask them to start searching in their territorial waters for the missing aircraft. Not long after this, at approximately 4 a.m. to 5 a.m., the general manager for the Upali operations in Malaysia, P.G.S. Jayawardene, received a phone call from Sellahewa, the production manager of the Upali Company in Singapore, asking him for the telephone number of a commander in the Malaysian Navy. Sellahewa informed the general manager that their boss, Wijewardene, and others were missing in the Upali Learjet as it had not reached Colombo.

The civilian aviation authorities in Malaysia and Indonesia initiated a comprehensive search and rescue operation involving the use of minesweepers in the territorial waters of both countries. Also, involved in the search from the air was a Royal Malaysian Air Force (RMAF) C-130 Hercules and a maritime reconnaissance aircraft.

Jayawardene made his way to Kuala Lumpur and met two Upali executives from Sri Lanka, Murugiah and Gunawardene, who had just arrived from Colombo. The three men decided to head to Indonesia to get as close to the likely crash site as possible. They arrived in Medan on 19 February and met the two men in charge of the Indonesian search and rescue operation; Mr Salamat, the Director of Civil Aviation, and a military representative, Major Sujiarto. While the two men in charge of the search operations could give no definite news to the Upali executives, they were shown a pack of letters written in Japanese and wrapped in tinfoil. Gunawardene inspected them but said they were nothing to do with the Upali aircraft. They had possibly come from a passing ship.

The following day, the three men went to the search and rescue office, where they were given a briefing on the search operation. On 21 February, Jayawardene contacted Major Sujiarto to see if there was any update and they were advised that the major had gone on an important mission. Sujiarto had in fact been called to a small fishing village named Tanjung Balai. Two days earlier, on the night of 19 February, a fisherman had arrived back from a trip and handed in a wheel. This was an intriguing development and Jayawardene contacted Sujiarto immediately. Sujiarto gave Jayawardene identification numbers on the wheel. Jayawardene duly made a note of these and then contacted Gunawardene at Upali in Singapore, where he had returned from Medan that morning. Jayawardene asked him to get in touch with Stillwell Aviation in Singapore to check the numbers. Stillwell Aviation confirmed that not only was the wheel from the Upali Learjet N482U, but specifically it was the outboard right-hand one that had been changed and refitted as the spare.

The identification of the wheel led to the search being intensified. The wheel had been found between the fishing village islands of Tanjung Balai and Pulau Salanama in the Straits of Malacca. One of the problems faced by any searchers in this area was that it was an extremely busy shipping route with large quantities of rubbish and other items deposited daily and found floating on the surface and washed up on shore. Any other items from the missing jet could easily be missed as either just rubbish or tangled up with floating debris. Nevertheless, it was a highly significant find and Jayawardene decided to go to Tanjung Balai and meet the fishermen for himself to see what other information they may have. Before he left, Jayawardene had made further enquiries and found that fishermen in the nearby village may have seen and heard something on the night the Learjet disappeared.

On 24 February, the Indonesian Navy prepared to make a thorough search of the area where the wheel was found. Also on that day, Jayawardene left for the villages with two companions and called in first at Tanjung Berinjin, which had an Indonesian Army command post. The officer in charge was 2nd Lt Sharill Attachi, who was extremely helpful and gave Jayawardene a briefing on the information he had gathered from the fishermen. It was clear that the Indonesian authorities had made every effort to assist in whatever way they could. 2nd Lt Attachi introduced Jayawardene and his companions to the lieutenant colonel in charge of the district at the district capital, Tebing Tengy. He had also arranged for Jayawardene to meet the fishermen concerned so he could question them himself. Jayawardene met the six fishermen in the fishing village of Verdage. Three of them in particular had quite specific information on what they had seen and heard. The first spoken to, Haroon, explained that on the night of 13 February he had heard a noise in the sky. He looked up and saw a light of some kind coming down. He described the noise he heard as being like that of an engine when it keeps 'missing' and then he heard an explosion at sea level. After the object hit the sea, he said there were large waves that rocked their fishing boats. Haroon went on to say that the following morning he went down to the sea and noticed some large objects floating on the surface. These were like glass and around 100m (328ft) away from where he was. He also said that he had seen cotton wool with blood-like substances floating.

Haroon described quite specifically where he was and the immediate area of where the object had come down in the sea. That night the boat he was on was stationary in relation to the islands of Pulau Barhala, Pulau Pandai and Pulau Salanama. He then stood and faced the direction he said he was facing to observe the object, which was to the east. Haroon said that in relation to the coast, he was in a boat that was in front of the village of Pagurawa, so the island of Pulau Barhala would have been to his 11 o'clock and one of the other islands was in front of him to the east at about 2 to 3 o'clock. He could not tell at what distance the object hit the sea in front of him but said it must have been fairly close because the waves from it rocked his boat. Haroon had been in a boat that belonged to a fisherman named Damin, but Damin himself was in another boat to the south at the time.

Damin also gave specific details of his location in relation to the three previously mentioned islands, so Jayawardene and his companions could get a good idea of the location of where the object came down. Damin said that on the night of 13 February, while they were in their boats, one of the fishermen shouted to him and pointed at the sky. He looked up in the direction where the fisherman was pointing. To start with, he heard and saw nothing, then he heard three explosions. The first two sounded as if they were in the air and the third was when the object hit the water. After the object hit, the boat Damin was in was rocked by large waves. Damin also stated that he then saw a red flame coming down from the east to the west and falling into the sea. He described this a being as large as a window.

Damin clarified his position relative to where he had seen the flaming object come down. He said the crash took place in front of him to the east and that it was very roughly 1km (0.62 mile) away. In relation to the coast, he described it as 12 o'clock to the north of Sipare-Pare, which was a coastal fishing area. Although the Malacca Straits are quite deep, Damin said that the depth of the sea where the object had come down was only around 12m (39ft). Damin had made his way over to the area for a look but could find nothing floating on the sea. The following morning Damin took his boat out to the fishing area for another look. When he arrived at the location, he found what looked like some kind of door floating on the sea. He said that there was a section of glass in it as if it was a door with a window. He described the floating object as being entirely blue in colour with red and white stripes around the glass.

The third fisherman to be questioned, Alhamsha, was described by Jayawardene as 'not a very intelligent person' who was unable to describe the location of the boat at the time. Nevertheless, Alhamsha said he had been resting in his boat when he heard a noise like a machine gun with a loud noise at the end of it. By the time he got up to have a look, it was all over. Alhamsha then described how the following day he made his way back to the area of sea where he had heard the noise to have a look. He saw two objects floating in the water. He described the first as being almost like glass and as big as a door. The second object interested him and he described it as quite large with a 'folded effect' with screws on the outer edge. He further described the front edge of the object as having a 'broken effect' and the whole object as having white, blue and red colours with a design of stripes coming around the curved side of the object. The inside of the object appeared to have an aluminium colour. Alhamsha had moved his boat close to the object and he tried to pull it out of the water but he cut himself on the jagged edges and dropped it. Jayawardene noticed the lacerations on Alhamsha's hands as he was talking.

After the meeting with the fishermen, Jayawardene wondered why they had not noticed any lighter debris, which must have been fairly close to the larger floating pieces that they had described. He also had the feeling that the three men had got together beforehand to decide how they were going to tell their story as each was trying to correct the other as they gave their individual accounts.

Jayawardene was also given a fully prepared plan that showed the location of the island, the main shipping routes, the flight path of the Learjet and the locations of where the fishing boats had stopped, as well as the rough area where the jet was believed to have come down. After mulling over everything he had seen and heard, Jayawardene was of the opinion that the fishermen had seen something coming down fast from the sky followed by an explosion, but that the rest of what he heard came from their imagination.

Three days later, on 27 February, Jayawardene met Mohammed Yamin, the head of the fishermen. Yamin had been further out from the land than the other fishermen. He was close to the shipping lanes in the Malacca Straits. Because he was that much further out, he was unable to use any visual references of land and the coastline to describe what he had seen and could only guess. However, he could indicate the island of Pulau Berhala on a compass drawing between 12 and 1 o'clock north. Yamin described seeing what he said looked like a meteor coming down very fast from east to west and hitting the water. He changed his description of the meteor to looking more like a *bintang* (Indonesian for a star). Yamin said there were two explosions but no waves. He could not tell if the explosions took place above the water or when the object hit the sea but said the explosions were so loud he instinctively looked at the fuel tank on his boat. Yamin's view of events was that the other three fishermen were exaggerating what they had seen.

Part of the problem facing Jayawardene and the searchers was that they still had a large area to cover to find anything because the information was so imprecise. When the information was compared with the radar details at the Malaysian Butterworth Air Force Base it was found that this area of sea had already been searched. The area had been searched according to the boundary of a circle and it made Jayawardene wonder if the aircraft had possibly come down outside the circle further to the east. Matters weren't helped when Major Sujiarto sent his officers to speak to the fishermen to try and pinpoint the area more accurately because they came up with three different points. The search and rescue personnel began to have serious doubts about the testimonies of the fishermen. Even though a rough area could be said to have been indicated, this was vast and was compounded by the deep waters in the Malacca Straits and fast-flowing currents.

In an effort to try and pinpoint the area more precisely, on the following day, 28 February, the Upali Singapore production manager, Sellahewa, made his way to Medan to try and learn more about the Learjet wheel and whether anything else may have been seen or heard. Sellahewa had regular involvement in liaising with Stillwell Aviation in Singapore regarding any maintenance issues with the Learjet, so he knew the background. He had originally arrived in Indonesia from Singapore on 20 February to join the Upali management team there to see if he could assist in any way. He learned that the wheel had become tangled in a fishing net about 10 miles (16km) south of the island of Pulau Berhala, which was located in Indonesian waters in the Straits of Malacca. Sellahewa ascertained that none of the fishermen had heard any noise of an explosion on the night of 13 February. His view was that the wheel had become detached as a result of an impact rather than an explosion. The wheel had bolts and a yellow metal bracket fitted. There were several identification numbers on the tyre and bracket. On the tyre was imprinted 'GOODYEAR Flight Eagle 17.5 x 5.75-8' with a laceration across the 'G' of 'GOODYEAR'. There was evidence of great forces on the wheel because the yellow metal bracket was dented and damaged. There were seven projections on one side of the wheel used in connection with the brakes. One of these had been completely wrenched off and three of the others had been damaged and dented. The spare wheel had been fitted to the right-hand side of the fuselage at the rear of the aircraft in the non-pressurised area. The fact that the Learjet was believed to have been in a nose dive and the spare wheel was fitted to the rear shows the tremendous impact that was sustained with the damage to the bracket and wheel. Nobody on board would have stood the slightest chance of surviving.

Minesweepers and naval divers searched as much as possible of the area indicated by the fishermen but nothing else was found. The main problem was the strength of the currents that hindered the search and would have carried any debris from the crash away from the area. Eventually the search was scaled down after nothing more was found.

The scope of the investigation took in the accident record of the Learjet, the prototype of which first flew in 1963. N482U was the tenth loss of a Learjet 35, although the accident record is not as bad as some try to suggest. The aviation side of the Upali organisation, Upali Air, had been formed in 1968 and was Sri Lanka's first domestic airline. An associate company (Upali Travels Limited) was formed in 1983 by Philip Wijewardene to provide aircraft and helicopters for corporate travel for the Upali group and to also be available for general hire and charter by outside companies and parties. By 1983 the small fleet consisted of the Learjet 35A N482U, a DH Twin Otter, two Cessnas (a 152 and a 206) and a Bell 206 helicopter. Although it formed part of the Upali fleet, the Learjet was not only registered in the USA but was owned by an American company, Upali USA Inc. It had been bought from Heli Orient Pte, Singapore, for US$3,770,390 using a loan from ARMCO-Pacific in Singapore. The actual ownership of the aircraft appears to have been shrouded in the same mystery that coloured all the other Upali Group's business dealings. The registered ownership was split between the financiers and Upali USA. Upali (USA) Inc. had a registered address of 'No 1, World Trade Centre, New York', whereas ARMCO-Pacific was Singapore-based and had only been formed two years prior to the purchase of the aircraft. The aircraft was delivered on 25 June 1982. Despite the price of the luxury aircraft, one thing the Upali jet did not have was proper toilet facilities. The toilets were under the seats and could be brought up for use. The decision to buy this particular aircraft was taken because of its greater range than the previous Upali company jet, a Cessna Citation II. The Learjet had a range of 2,289 miles (3,684km) and could seat eight passengers. The possibility of waiting for the upgraded version of the Citation, the III, with greater range than the previous model was decided against and so it was Learjet 35A N482U that had awaited its passengers and crew on the apron area in front of the Wira Kris hangar at Kuala Lumpur's Subang airport on the evening of 13 February 1983.

The chief pilot for Upali Air was Yogendran Selladurai (not to be confused with Selladurai, the driver mentioned earlier) and he had flown the Learjet to Sri Lanka after it was purchased in June 1982. He said to the investigators that he had 175 hours flying time on N482U and had experienced no major problems with the aircraft. The investigation found that in the days leading up to the disappearance of the aircraft, there were two sets of maintenance issues in Singapore and Kuala Lumpur. In Singapore, Stillwell Aviation (Pte) Ltd was the agent for Gates Learjet Aircraft and a subsidiary of Stillwell Aviation Ltd in Australia.

N482U had been with the Upali organisation for six and a half months before it disappeared. The aircraft had made seventeen flights, with the first taking place on 26 July 1982. The majority were in and out of Kuala Lumpur and the destinations included Hong Kong, Singapore, Penang, Perth (Australia), Darwin, Cocos Islands, Sydney, Melbourne and Colombo. Despite being registered in the USA, the jet had not made one trip there during the time it was with the company, although that was not unusual.

There were three pilots working for the Upali group who had undertaken training in Tucson, Arizona, and who were qualified to fly the aircraft. These were Yogendran, Anandappa and de Zoysa (Anandappa and de Zoysa were flying the jet on the night it disappeared). Other than the wheel and the damaged bracket that had been found by the fisherman, there was no other wreckage for the investigation to focus on. It was left to speculate and try to examine what may have gone wrong with the aircraft that caused it to overspeed and fall from the sky to the sea in twenty-two seconds. The two pilots were fully trained and qualified. Two possible causes were human error, or Anandappa falling ill and de Zoysa having to pull him off the controls, causing a loss of control, but the latter was unlikely as both had recently passed their medicals. Also, despite the fact that it was reported co-pilot de Zoysa had to cut short his training in Tucson due to personal problems, he was nevertheless qualified to US Federal Aviation Administration standard to fly as co-pilot on the jet. The weather was not considered a factor in the disappearance either as it was a clear and calm night with no turbulence or thunderstorms.

That then left two main areas to consider: a possible catastrophic defect or sabotage. The possible defects considered included a problem with elevator control, sudden decompression and any other possible mechanical or electrical problems that would make the aircraft uncontrollable. If the control cable for the elevator had snapped or jammed, it could have caused the aircraft to nose dive and it would have taken a considerable effort to operate the controls to pull it out of this. A sudden depressurisation of the aircraft would also have caused serious problems as the pilots would fall unconscious in well under a minute. There are a number of examples of pilots becoming unconscious due to hypoxia in various aircraft, including a Learjet. Two examples show similarities to the Upali jet incident. These were: the crash of Learjet 35 N47BA on 25 October 1999 and the Helios Airways Boeing 737-31S 5B-DBY crash in August 2005. The Helios 737 crash is of particular interest because in the case of this aircraft and the Upali Learjet, both had reported previous door problems and there had been issues with the air conditioning. Also, both aircraft appeared to hit their difficulties at roughly the same height – 29,800ft (9,083m) in the case of the Helios 737, and just above 27,500ft (8,382m) in the Upali Learjet.

Major inspections and maintenance of N482U were carried out at Stillwell Aviation in Melbourne, Australia, with the last major test being when the aircraft had completed 150 hours' flying time. Smaller maintenance issues were dealt with by Singapore General Aviation Services Company (SINGAS). The engineers were well trained and fully licensed, having attended courses in the USA on the aircraft's Garrett TFE731 engines. There were, however, two separate groups of issues concerning maintenance on the aircraft. Some of the problems were rectified and some were not.

On 31 January 1983, ten days before the aircraft disappeared, Anandappa flew the Learjet from Colombo to Kuala Lumpur. On arrival he sent a telex to Stillwell Aviation, the Learjet agents in Singapore, and advised that during the course of his flight he noticed a number of problems to which attention was needed. The items he listed were: the Mach trim system was unserviceable; the autopilot, vertical speed, airspeed and altitude hold were unserviceable; the radar T/X (transmitter) and indicator needed to be refitted after repairs in Melbourne; the distance measuring equipment (DME) receiver needed to be replaced after repair by Aero Systems Inc.; the hour meter (Hobbs meter) was five hours slow and needed to be advanced by five hours; a replacement display screen for the cabin which showed flight information to be installed; the cabin environmental system was always cold regardless of hot or cold selection and whether the selection was done manually or automatically; the co-pilot's attitude indicator was unserviceable; and the ITT (the Interstage Turbine Temperature, which was the temperature of the exhaust gases between the high-pressure and the low-pressure turbines) fluctuated on the right-hand (starboard) engine.

The Learjet was flown from Kuala Lumpur to SINGAS at Seletar airport in Singapore on 9 February, four days before its penultimate flight. On its arrival, two engineers were assigned to attend to the list of defects highlighted by Anandappa. Over a period of two days, the defects were attended to with input and suggestions from the Stillwell service manager in Melbourne. Three replacement items had to be flown up to Singapore from the Stillwell stores in Melbourne. These were an air data sensor, the cabin screen displaying flight information and the radar T/X (transmitter) and indicator. They arrived on Thursday, 10 February, the day after the Learjet's arrival in Singapore and were duly fitted.

One item from the list of defects that could not be rectified at the time was the co-pilot's attitude indicator. It was removed from the aircraft and sent to the Gates Learjet Corporation in the USA for replacement. In the meantime, the electrical connection was secured by a blank plate covering the hole. Once the work was finished on 10 February, the aircraft's engines were started and all the systems and repairs were checked by Anandappa, the two engineers and the market development manager for Stillwell Aviation, Singapore. The following day Anandappa took off from Seletar in the aircraft and took it up to 37,000ft (11,277m) for a flight test. The test went fairly well but two problems still remained. The aircraft radar did not function very well at high altitude and, perhaps more significantly, there remained a problem with the environmental system as it was still not functioning and the temperature in the aircraft was far from comfortable.

The day following the test flight over the South China Sea, Anandappa and co-pilot de Zoysa flew back to Kuala Lumpur from Singapore with two passengers. This was the day before the fateful flight. On his arrival in Kuala Lumpur, Anandappa sent a message to the Stillwell Aviation Market Development Manager in Singapore and informed him that he considered the radar to be alright but the environmental system was still a problem and not functioning well. He said that the temperature was very uncomfortable.

On the final day (13 February), the Stillwell Aviation market development manager, Tom Boyd, flew up to Kuala Lumpur, arriving at 11.45 a.m. He was met by two members of Wira Kris Pte, the Learjet handling agent, and taken straight to the aircraft, which was parked on the apron outside the Wira Kris facility. A ground power unit, a nitrogen bottle and compressed air bottles were provided, and they set to work on the temperature control valve on the aircraft. As they were completing the work, Anandappa and Copilot de Zoysa arrived. Anandappa climbed on board and then started the right engine to test the valve. This was being checked by Boyd, who said that the valve was working.

Once the work was complete, Boyd asked if there were any other issues that needed looking at. Anandappa mentioned the flight information display screen, which he had flagged up on his original list of problems after his flight from Colombo to Kuala Lumpur on 31 January. This was checked and was now found to be working correctly. Boyd then went into the aft compartment of the aircraft for a security check and also to ensure that it was free of any foreign objects such as misplaced tools. Once he was satisfied it was clear, he secured the panel doors and made an entry in the log book.

After the disappearance of the aircraft, Yogendran was asked if he had any comments about mechanical defects with the aircraft. He referred to the issue regarding the non-functioning co-pilot's attitude indicator (ADI) and said that in a commercial airliner such a fault would prevent a flight going ahead as it is considered a prime flight instrument.

Without the wreckage of the Learjet to examine, it was impossible to arrive at a firm conclusion as to the cause of the crash. It also left open the possibility that it could have been brought down by sabotage or a bomb, or just a catastrophic mechanical failure of some kind. If it was a bomb or sabotage, the questions were open as to whether it was a grudge or some kind of political or business rivalry, or possibly one or more persons who stood to gain from the assets and money held outside Sri Lanka by the Upali group.

Leaving aside Wijewardene's considerable business holdings inside Sri Lanka, the set-up of the Upali Group overseas resembled a complex chess puzzle of interlinked companies and directors that was so tangled as to make it appear that all the companies and business interests were autonomous, yet at the same time locked into each other.

The bottom line of this complex arrangement was that while he was in Sri Lanka, Philip Wijewardene could almost say in all honesty that he had virtually no business interests outside the country and neither did he benefit much from what little there was on paper. There is nothing new about a businessman wanting to reduce his tax bill; the practice went on long before Wijewardene was born and it still goes on in the twenty-first century. What made Wijewardene's case slightly different was that it could be inferred that the overseas investments and businesses actually benefitted others inside Sri Lanka besides Wijewardene himself. If this was the case, then who those others might be can only be guessed at.

Could there have been a reason to kill some or all of the people on board the aircraft? Of the crew, Captain Sydney de Zoysa and acting steward Athula Senanayake were found to lead relatively quiet lives and both were politically neutral. Sydney de Zoysa had been a commercial pilot with Air Ceylon. When the airline went into liquidation in 1979 as a result of severe financial difficulties, de Zoysa was not absorbed into the new national carrier, Air Lanka. Outside of the new national airline and the Sri Lankan Air Force, there were not many opportunities for pilots and de Zoysa was fortunate to land himself a job as a co-pilot with Wijewardene's aviation company, Upali Travels Limited. His personal life was difficult in that his wife had been killed in a car accident and their two sons and a daughter were being brought up by his wife's sister. With the disappearance/death of de Zoysa himself, the children had therefore lost both parents in separate tragic circumstances. De Zoysa was said to have no known enemies according to those who knew him; the same was also said of acting steward and 'Man Friday' Senanayake.

The captain, Noel Anandappa, was a somewhat different character to the other two crew members. He was married, without children and had served in the Sri Lankan Air Force. On his retirement, he had joined Upali Travels Limited as a captain/pilot. He was considered to be a reserved man and did not associate with many people, although he maintained a close link with a squadron leader from the Air Force. Despite being described as a man with a reserved nature, it is alleged that Anandappa did not get on very well with a couple of people. At the time of the disappearance of the Upali Learjet, Anandappa was in the process of being ejected from his residence in Hendala, Sri Lanka. The man who was kicking him out of the rented property was the owner. The circumstances appear to be that the owner wanted Anandappa out of his property, but Anandappa wasn't prepared to go, which had forced the owner to file an ejectment case in the District Court of Colombo. It was alleged that the two were 'not well disposed towards each other'. The other person that Anandappa did not get on well with was his sibling. Although these are only two examples, it could be taken that he was not necessarily an easy person to get along with. His family were politically involved and supported Sri Lanka's United National Political Party, which was right-leaning and tended to represent the interests of the business community and landed gentry.

Both pilots had been medically examined by Dr Upali de Mel at the University of Sri Lanka's Faculty of Medicine on its Colombo campus and they had been declared fit for the renewal of their pilot's licences. There appeared to be nothing in the background of the pilots to raise any suspicions. The next stage was to look at who may have wanted to cause the Learjet to crash.

If the aircraft came down as a result of sabotage or a bomb, then who could have been responsible for it? The first group that automatically springs to mind is the much-feared Tamil Tigers (Liberation Tigers of Tamil Eelam or LTTE), which had been formed in May 1976 to fight for a separate Tamil homeland in the north and east of Sri Lanka. The real trouble with the Tamil Tigers did not begin until 1983 with the start of the Sri Lankan civil war, which was the same year Wijewardene's Learjet disappeared. However, prior to that, there had been a low-level insurgency against government targets such as policemen and politicians, characterised by what was to become the Tamil Tigers' trademark of extreme violence. However, despite the lower intensity of earlier Tamil Tiger attacks on government targets, they did bomb a Sri Lankan airliner four and a half years before the loss of Wijewardene's Learjet. On Thursday, 7 September 1978, an HS 748 registered 4R-ACJ belonging to the then national airline, Air Ceylon, was sitting on the apron at Ratmalana, Colombo's old main airport. The twin tur-boprop airliner was about to depart to Katunayake, the main international airport for the country, on a posi-tioning flight to pick up passengers for a flight to the Maldives. As the captain and co-pilot went through their preflight checks, they heard a loud explosion. A bomb had been placed in the middle of the fuselage that

Sri Lankan Multi-Millionaire

Gates Learjet 35A N81MR, similar to the one belonging to Philip Upali Wijewardene. (*Fred Seggie*)

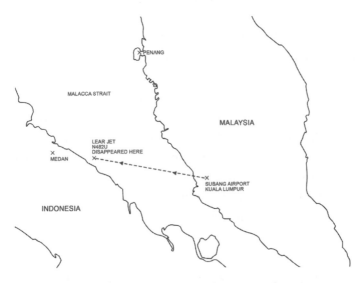

The route taken by Wijewardene's Learjet after leaving Subang Airport, Kuala Lumpur, to a point close to the Indonesian coastline. (*bhardwaz – FIVERR*)

caused a fire, damaging the aircraft beyond repair, but fortunately with no casualties. The Tamil Tigers claimed responsibility for the attack, although there was speculation that extremist Sinhalese had placed the bomb so as to implicate the Tamils and create persecution by the government. The Tamil Tigers certainly didn't need anybody doing anything in their name as they were quite capable of doing it for themselves and the flight had arrived from Jaffna, the heartland of Tamil Tiger territory. Two young men who had boarded the flight at Jaffna were seen to linger after landing in the area where the bomb had gone off. They had waited until the flight attendants and all the passengers had disembarked before getting off themselves. By the time of the loss of the Learjet, the Tamil Tigers were much better organised as a terrorist group and would have been able to carry out such an attack as placing a bomb on the Learjet in Kuala Lumpur using a worldwide network of sympathisers and operatives.

Philip Wijewardene may have represented the Sinhalese establishment as a businessman, although there had been talk of him entering politics (as previously mentioned, the president was a cousin), but at the time of his disappearance, he was considered more as a businessman with some interest in maybe entering politics. Had his aircraft been targeted by the Tamil Tigers because he was a cousin of the president, it would have been expected that they would at least have claimed some kind of responsibility for the attack to show that they could strike at people who were close to the leadership of the country. However, there was no claim by the group after the disappearance of the Learjet and the general view is that the Tamil Tigers had nothing to do with the loss.

Comments were made by the Upali Singapore production manager that whilst Wijewardene appeared to have no known enemies in Malaysia and Singapore, he did have many political opponents in Sri Lanka and mentioned a senior Sri Lankan politican in particular being angry with Wijewardene because he felt he was causing him a political threat. This, of course, was only his opinion.

Had someone wanted to sabotage the Learjet, then the security procedures in place at the airport in Kuala Lumpur would not have been a great barrier to anyone wishing to gain access to the aircraft. It was possible to enter the secure area at the airport on the production of a passport or identity card. This was brought to light in the interview of the Upali driver Raju, who said that he had obtained a security pass into the secure zone of the airport and used it for the entire day without surrendering it at the gate when he left. He had picked up and dropped off the two Learjet pilots at the airport at 2.30 p.m. on the day of the flight. The theory that some kind of sabotage was responsible for the aircraft's disappearance also led to an investigation that looked at security at Kuala Lumpur's Subang Airport. It came to the conclusion that it was not completely secure, which left the possibility open that someone could have placed a bomb on the aircraft or sabotaged it in some way.

Although sabotage was ruled out, it was still a possibility, just as mechanical failure of some kind also remained a possibility. Without evidence from the wreckage on the seabed, it is impossible to say. The more cynical observers of this tragedy merely point to those who would stand to gain considerably if Philip Upali Wijewardene were to just disappear one day.

CHAPTER 5

MURDER, SUICIDE OR ACCIDENT?

Many would recognise the character of Belgian business-man Alfred Loewenstein of the early twentieth century as being in the same mould as latter-day bond traders and hedge fund managers who make and lose huge sums of money. In terms of wealth he can be compared with the billionaire technocrats of the early twenty-first century. He had an eye for minute detail and he knew how to turn a buck.

Alfred Loewenstein was born in Brussels, Belgium, in 1877. His father, Bernard, was German and had been a minor player in banking in Belgium, after marrying the daughter of a Belgian banker. Following his father's lead, Loewenstein junior started off in business finance in his early twenties. Alfred's father was bankrupted during a downturn and Alfred struggled to keep going, but he managed to keep his head above water and recovered sufficiently enough to embark on a career in which he never looked back.

What had helped Alfred Loewenstein's business career to really take off was his involvement with two busi-nessmen on the other side of the Atlantic. These were an American named Frederick S. Pearson, an electrical engineer, and a Canadian, William Mackenzie, a railway contractor and entrepreneur, who is recognised as the 'father' of the Canadian railroad system. Both Pearson and Mackenzie were risk-takers and were prepared to gamble on a large scale. In Loewenstein they found exactly the same type of personality as themselves on the financial side. What they were initially looking for from Loewenstein was someone who could provide capital for their South American business ventures. They had formed a company named Brazilian Traction and were looking to build a tramway in Rio de Janeiro. Loewenstein found that he had a gift for raising the finance and, not only that, he also found he had a gift for manipulating the financial press to his benefit as well. One thing that the Belgian did do to please both investors and Pearson and Mackenzie was to introduce bearer bonds, which hid the identity of the investors. These bonds proved to be immensely popular, so much so that the investors couldn't get enough of them. The end result was that that money poured in for Brazilian Traction. It was a fruitful partnership and a couple of years later, in 1908, Loewenstein again was able to come to the rescue with additional finance from Europe.

Although he had many business interests in the course of his career, he took a particular interest in artificial silk manufacturing in its early days. In conjunction with a Canadian businessman, James Dunn, the two of them invested in British Celanese and this made a huge profit for the time of more than £1 million.

In 1926 Loewenstein established a company that he would use as the main vehicle for his investment ventures. This was the International Holding and Investment

Company Ltd and the experience he gained in raising finance for the Rio Tramway led him to become deeply involved in a number of other similar companies including the Barcelona Traction Light and Power Company, the Hydro Electric Securities Corporation, the Mexican Light and Power Company and the Mexican Tramways Company.

Loewenstein's rapid accumulation of wealth and his reputation as a financier was such that he was eventually believed to be richer than the Rothschilds and arms dealer Sir Basil Zaharoff.

Not long before he died, Loewenstein had offered a loan to the Belgian government for the colossal amount for the time of £10 million, interest free for one year. He was said to be bitterly disappointed by the rejection of the offer.

For all his wealth, many found him aloof and difficult to get on with. His obituary in *The Times* mentioned that he disliked opposition of any kind and didn't take well to criticism, although that could be said about many more people than just Loewenstein. His response, though, could be quite extreme, which made business and personal relationships difficult. He tended to focus intensely on the smallest detail of whatever piece of business he was working on and in many ways this intensity and focus made him a solitary figure and he only looked for cooperation from others when he absolutely needed it. His obituary also mentioned wild mood swings from the depths of depression to the heights of optimism, which suggest he may have been a manic depressive, although this has never been declared outright.

Despite the negative portrayals, *The Times* obituary also mentioned that despite his awkward character Loewenstein was known to be loyal and generous to those who were near to him and worked for him. It also suggested that he had some self-awareness of his shortcomings in his personal dealings, but he was also unforgiving of people with whom he had issues. Although they acknowledged his undoubted drive and business skills, the various obituary notices were hardly glowing character references. They painted a picture of someone who was stubborn, cantankerous and held grudges against those who crossed him in any way. In addition, he neither smoked nor drank as he believed it impaired his mental capacities. He was also a devout Catholic. Besides his dominating interest in business, he did take a great interest in horses, both for racing and hunting. Although he travelled a great deal and had homes on the Continent, he spent the majority of his time in England and owned the Pinfold Estate near Thorpe Satchville in Leicestershire. Here, both he and his wife entertained the gentry and took part in the local hunts including the Quorn, Cottesmore and Belvoir.

Loewenstein's relationship with his wife Madeleine was described by those who worked for him as rather distant. In many ways the marriage appeared to be more of a working arrangement rather than a tempestuous meeting of two like-minded individuals. At the time of their wedding she was twenty and he was thirty-two. Madeleine was born Madeleine Berthe Helene Marie Missone in 1888 and came from an upper-class Belgian family. She married Loewenstein in August 1908 and they had one child, a son, Robert Serge. Although they led separate lives and slept in separate bedrooms, Alfred travelled a great deal in the course of his business, so it was not unreasonable that Madeleine would prefer to stay behind and run the properties they owned in Brussels, Biarritz and Thorpe Satchville.

Loewenstein was forward looking in many ways and he could see the time-saving advantages of commercial air travel, particularly owning his own aircraft. There was great interest in air travel by the mid 1920s and Loewenstein can be said to be a pioneer in executive air travel with his own aircraft. He owned a number of different aircraft over the years and he had been particularly keen to buy a new aircraft that had come onto the market and fit it out to his own specifications. The aircraft that he wanted to use for his business travel was a Fokker F.VII B/3m. The 'B' version had an increased wing area and more powerful engines (an increase from 200hp per engine to 220hp per engine) over the earlier 'A' model. It was constructed with a steel tube fuselage covered in fabric with a wing that was covered in plywood. There were three engines with one on each wing and one in the nose. The first flight took place on 24 November 1924 and the type was bought by a number of airlines including Dutch airline KLM, Belgian airline Sabena and the Polish airline LOT. There were also a number of different variants used by military forces.

To his great satisfaction, the brand-new aircraft was duly delivered, completely fitted out to his requirements, to Croydon Airport in the middle of June 1928. His enthusiasm for air travel was undiminished by an incident that had occurred only the previous month. He had been on a business tour of the USA in a hired Fokker Trimotor and had been invited to Philadelphia by the investment company, Drexel & Co. On 5 May, the hired Trimotor duly landed at Philadelphia Airport with Loewenstein and his entourage. Investment banker and a partner in Drexel & Co., Edward T. 'Ned' Stotesbury, had arranged a rather grand welcome for Loewenstein with a welcoming speech to be made and photographs to be taken afterwards. While this was all being set up as the aircraft came to a stop and the passengers got out onto the apron, Loewenstein was wandering around and walked under the wing at an angle and passed right through the blades of one of the propellers. The engines had been turned off but the propellers were slowing down and still turning. Although he had passed right through the turning blades, one of them caught the back of his hat and sent it flying. While he may not have been killed had the blade struck his head, it could have caused a serious injury. The event didn't seem to unduly bother him and moments later he was being photographed next to Stotesbury, seemingly none the worse for wear.

After the US visit, Loewenstein returned to Britain and in early July, he needed to travel over to Brussels to attend to business there. It was an ideal opportunity to use the still fairly new Fokker, registered G-EBYI.

On Wednesday, 4 July, Loewenstein and his group arrived at Croydon Airport at around 6 p.m. for their flight to Brussels. Croydon was the Heathrow of its time and was the base for Imperial Airways flights. Loewenstein's aircraft had been towed out from its hangar and made ready for the trip. While the others boarded, Loewenstein quickly went into the terminal building. He emerged a few minutes later and climbed on board. The plane left Croydon at 6.45 p.m. and everyone settled down for the trip to Haren Airport, Brussels.

The pilot was Donald Drew, who was employed by Imperial Airways as a captain by Imperial Airways and seconded as a personal pilot to Loewenstein. Drew was highly regarded and before joining Imperial his earlier flying career included the Royal Flying Corps (RFC), and he specialised in flying seaplanes. Drew cut a dashing figure and was sought after by the wealthy to fly aircraft on tours and on longer, arduous flights where his flying skills and experience were useful. An example of this was an extended 12,000-mile (19,312km) trip he made in early 1929 to Karachi for Mrs A.S. Cleaver, the wife of a colonel and the daughter of the Northern Ireland finance minister H.M. Pollock. Drew flew Mrs Cleaver's own Gipsy Moth and the trip was purely for sightseeing.

One quality about Drew stood out from the rest and that was his reserve. He was sought after by the wealthy and titled to fly their aircraft because they could rely on his discretion. This is not to say that such people were engaged in nefarious activities, but most of them valued their privacy. After he had flown the new Imperial Airways Short S.8 Calcutta flying boat G-AATZ from Rochester down to Athens, Drew's general air of discretion was described by an aviation journalist as 'the proverbial shut oyster'. After much coaxing and questioning, the journalist was able to get a few words out of Drew to describe the flight and the aircraft. As one of Imperial Airways' most experienced pilots, he was a natural first choice to be put forward for ad hoc flights for holidays and tours. Although working for Imperial, he was available to fly for Loewenstein as and when he was required.

Besides Drew and Loewenstein himself, there were five other people on board the flight. These were: Fred Baxter, who was Loewenstein's valet; Arthur Hodgson, Loewenstein's male secretary; Paula Bidalon and Eileen Clarke, both stenographers; and finally Robert Little, the mechanic. It seemed a large party for a short trip across the Channel, but Baxter accompanied Loewenstein everywhere and so did Hodgson, who was his closest confidante as much as he was his secretary. The two stenographers (one to take dictation in French and one in English) were also regularly in attendance wherever Loewenstein went and he was in the habit of calling for a stenographer sometimes in the middle of the night in a hotel as he was constantly at work at all hours of the day and night.

The early part of the flight was uneventful enough. The aircraft flew out across Kent from Croydon, crossed the coastline and went out over the English Channel. There are conflicting reports about what Loewenstein was doing during this part of the trip. It was said by those on board that he was reading a book, even though Loewenstein rarely read books. As the aircraft started to get closer to the French coast, Loewenstein reportedly marked the place in the book he was reading and stood up from his seat. He wanted to go to the toilet and as he made his way to the back of the aircraft, he and Hodgson (his male secretary) spoke together briefly, after which Loewenstein then opened the door from the cabin and went into the toilet. After some time had lapsed, Hodgson became concerned that Loewenstein had not reappeared and he went to see if he was alright, thinking he may be ill. When he found the toilet and rear vestibule area by the door were empty, he immediately went to tell Drew, the pilot, that Loewenstein was missing from the aircraft. In all the numerous accounts of Hodgson finding Loewenstein gone, there is not one mention of whether the main door leading to the outside of the aircraft was open or unfastened.

It was a stunning announcement to make and the only conclusion was that he had somehow fallen out of the aircraft to his certain death. Drew brought the Fokker down and made a landing on the beach at Fort-Mardyck in France. This was a restricted military area and soldiers were quickly on the scene in reaction to the amazing sight of a plane appearing almost as if from nowhere, with a party of distraught people on board telling them that their boss had fallen out of the aircraft into the Channel.

It was obvious to the officer in charge at Fort-Mardyck that there was no security issue, but that something extraordinary had happened, so he ordered the release of the aircraft and its occupants. Drew took off from the beach and landed at Saint-Inglevert aerodrome, which was only a few minutes further flying time on from the beach. The whole group, including Drew, went on to stay at the Hotel Metropole in Calais, where they arrived at 5 a.m. the following morning. Shortly after their arrival there they were all interviewed by the authorities.

Loewenstein's wife, Madeleine, was at their main residence in Rue de la Science in Brussels when she was informed of his fall from the aircraft. She dressed in mourning clothes and immediately set out for Calais by road. After meeting the rest of her husband's party at the Metropole, she assisted in organising a large search and offered a reward to whoever could find her husband's body. She then set off for the aerodrome at Saint-Inglevert with Drew. The Fokker had been parked there awaiting her arrival. She looked over the aircraft and inspected the interior. She found her husband's necktie and collar in the toilet. After she finished her inspection, she instructed Drew and Little to dispose of the plane, by which she meant sell it off. Drew and Little duly took the Fokker back to Croydon, following which they had been deputised by Madeleine to charter a vessel at Dover and go straight out into the Channel and help to search for Loewenstein's body. They chartered a Dover tug named *Lady Brassey* and went out to the area where Drew believed Loewenstein had fallen. However, after two days of searching there was no sign of the body and the *Lady Brassey* returned to Dover.

There were others also searching, helped no doubt, by the incentive of the reward money. A fisherman from the small fishing village of Bray-Dunes near Dunkirk and next to the Belgian border had stated, quite categorically, that he had seen a parachute coming down towards the sea on Wednesday, 4 July, the day of Loewenstein's disappearance. It was a few miles from where the fisherman was and he saw the parachute come down close to a boat. He explained that he did not feel the need to go out to investigate further or help as the parachute had come down so close to the boat. When this sighting was put to the Dunkirk Commissioner of Police by the British United Press Agency in a phone interview, the commissioner responded: 'The police here have heard of no report that a parachute was seen to descend from an aeroplane near here on the day on which Captain Loewenstein, the banker, was reported missing.'

He finished by saying: 'All we know is that when the plane landed, the occupants were in a state of excitement, which was obviously quite genuine.'

Other than the fisherman's sighting of the parachute, there was no other sighting nor mention of it.

The disappearance prompted a flurry of rumours and counter-rumours. One of these that prompted an official denial from the authorities at Dunkirk was the suggestion that Loewenstein's plane had made a clandestine landing at another point on the French coast prior to coming down on the beach at Fort-Mardyck. The story alleged that Loewenstein left the plane alone and made his way to Dunkirk, where he boarded the French steamer *Flamant*, which sailed for Tilbury that evening. Despite the unlikelihood of the suggestion, it was thoroughly checked out and the passport officers connected with the steamer's voyage at both ports were questioned, it being found that nobody resembling Loewenstein had been seen by them. The main point to refute the theory was that the timescale of the Fokker leaving Croydon and landing on the beach near Fort-Mardyck would not have allowed enough time for a landing and take-off at another point along the coast. The possibility that

Loewenstein may have left the plane on the beach by Fort-Mardyck and then made his way to Dunkirk from there was also refuted by a French soldier who observed the plane landing and watched it after it landed. The soldier said that at no point did anyone walk away from the plane until a contingent went down to investigate.

With the number of rumours being passed around and conjecture in the press, Madeleine Loewenstein felt compelled to issue a statement on the matter in which she said: 'The death of Mr Loewenstein is unhappily beyond doubt from the official investigations and the unanimity of the witnesses there is no question but that he embarked at Croydon, and that the aeroplane never landed except at Mardyck.'

The newspapers seemed happy enough at this point to support Madeleine's statement. Her brother also spoke to the newspapers, expressing his disbelief that there would be any chance of finding Loewenstein's body taking into account the height and speed that he fell from the plane.

The *Daily Herald* reported on 9 July 1928 that Madame Loewenstein had summoned all senior staff from London and Paris, plus staff from a number of other offices, to her chateau to discuss what had happened and to get an investigation under way. The newspaper reported that she had promptly struck down any suggestions that Loewenstein had faked his disappearance for some reason.

In order to try and obtain a death certificate in the absence of a body, an inquiry was arranged by Madeleine Loewenstein in Brussels on 9 July that necessitated the calling of a number of witnesses from Belgium and Britain, including the pilot Donald Drew. At this hearing

Drew stated that the aircraft door could be opened in flight. He also told the inquest that he thought he felt a shock when the plane was about 5 miles (8.04km) from the French coast.

There were suggestions in some quarters that Madeleine Loewenstein seemed in a bit of a hurry to get a death certificate issued by the authorities. The obvious implication was that she wanted to get her hands on the wealth as quickly as possible. Under Belgian law, in the absence of a body, it took four years from the date of a person disappearing for a death certificate to be issued in normal circumstances. Assuming that the accounts given by all those present on the aircraft at the time of his disappearance were genuine, it could be taken as reasonable proof that he was dead as nobody could survive a fall from 4,000ft (1,219m) onto water, which would be like hitting concrete from a great height. The counter-argument to Madeleine wanting to get her hands on the money is why shouldn't she? She was lawfully married to Alfred Loewenstein and although their relationship may have been rather formal, the marriage was not known to be in trouble and they were living together. Her husband had been a generous provider to her and she wanted for nothing. She had every legal right to try and expedite the formalities. Apart from anything else, she had several large and expensive properties to run along with the staff, so there were bills to pay and it would be difficult to try and keep it all going if she was denied access to the funds that were required.

On the day that Madeleine Loewenstein's brother spoke to the press to confirm Loewenstein was assuredly on the aircraft, a trawler left Dunkirk to search the sea off Gravelines near Calais. After searching the general area for some hours, they finally found Loewenstein's body floating in the sea 10 miles (16.09km) north of Cap Gris-Nez. The body was not in good condition and had started decomposing. The corpse was naked apart from underwear and socks. Loewenstein was identified by a gold watch wristlet holder he was wearing that had his name and address inscribed on the back. He also had an identity disc on a chain. Whilst it seemed strange that the body should have been found almost naked, it was believed that having fallen from such a great height, the force of hitting the water would have torn his clothes off.

The trawler took the body into Calais, where it was formally identified at the mortuary in Calais by his two brothers-in-law (Maitre Convert and Lieutenant Missone). The brothers-in-law also visited the crew of the trawler for details of the recovery and also assured them that they would be rewarded for their efforts. Madeleine Loewenstein was reported to be distraught at the news and had rushed from Brussels to Calais by car with her brothers.

The judicial authorities from Boulogne also travelled to Calais the day after the body was brought in by the fishermen. A celebrated pathologist named Dr Paul was appointed to carry out the post-mortem examination. Dr Paul was something of a local celebrity and had been become known to the general public when he was involved in carrying out the post mortem on a British nurse named

May Daniels the previous year. She had been murdered in Boulogne and it was a high-profile case at the time, which remains unsolved to this day. Dr Paul's autopsy report did not note anything untoward that was not consistent with Loewenstein's fall. There was a large wound on his stomach where his body had hit a rock. The autopsy also mentioned traces of alcohol, which was seized on by many as proof of something amiss as Loewenstein was strictly teetotal. However, the body produces small quantities of alcohol during the decomposition process and this is more than likely to what the autopsy report was referring.

After the body was found, Captain Iron, the Dover harbour master, gave a press interview in which he stated that on the day following Loewenstein's disappearance, 5 July, he had been requested by Madame Loewenstein to carry out a search of the area of the Channel where the plane had flown over. However, nothing was seen, but Captain Iron pointed out that they had not expected to see anything on account of a body sinking first and not rising to the surface for eight or nine days, which was, in fact, what happened.

The French board of enquiry decided not to make public any formal findings but did communicate with the Belgian and British authorities that their view was that Loewenstein had committed suicide rather than been involved in any kind of accident.

At the French enquiry, Donald Drew said that they had left Croydon at 6.45 p.m. and the first he knew of Captain Loewenstein's disappearance was when the valet, Fred Baxter, had banged on the glass partition separating the cockpit from the cabin with a piece of paper stating 'Captain gone'. Drew said he was 'amazed' and made to land on the sands at Fort-Mardyck as soon as he could.

The discovery of Loewenstein's body solved a number of pending problems, not least of which was the passing of the estate to his wife. However, whilst it solved some problems, it created another, namely how had a 51-year-old man managed to fall from a plane at 4,000ft (1,219m) without anybody inside the aircraft knowing about it?

With the announcement of Loewenstein's death, there was what was described as a hectic day on the London Stock Exchange, but at the end of trading things had settled down and the financial press reported the New York Stock Exchange coming in as a buyer. The frantic offloading of stocks and shares in Loewenstein's companies that was expected failed to materialise. There was also a reassuring statement issued by Loewenstein's International Holdings and the Hydro Electric Company Ltd that helped to calm the markets and the share price of both companies rallied by the end of the day.

The effect of Loewenstein's death on the financial world can best be summed up by part of an article in the *Daily Herald* that stated: '… his death has created a worldwide sensation, and so extensive and divergent were his interests that some very important branches of financial life are affected by it …'

The article went on to say that even the British turf had been affected as Loewenstein had maintained a keen interest in racing and the previous year had spent £7,000 on a horse called Easter Hero, of which he had great hopes for winning the Grand National.

The Paris Bourse issued a report that stated J. Henry Schroeder were assuming Loewenstein's financial arrangements with immediate effect. At the end of the day on the Bourse there was a drop of 300 Francs in the share price of one of Loewenstein's companies named Tubise. Overall, though, the situation could have been much worse but it was still precarious. Insurance policies had been taken out against Loewenstein's accidental death. The cover needed was so large that the risk was spread amongst several companies.

One area that was affected by Loewenstein's initial disappearance was the share price in some artificial silk manufacturers. A financial press report by the *Daily Herald*'s financial correspondent on 11 July stated that prior to his disappearance, the prices had been affected due to Loewenstein having been speculating quite heavily in their shares. Two were mentioned in the report: Glanxatoff, which was being quoted on the London Stock Exchange at £6 7s 6d a unit, and Enka, which was being quoted in Amsterdam at Fl457. The financial correspondent's view was that, despite Loewenstein's speculative moves in these shares, they remained a good buy and recommended them to potential purchasers. He also mentioned the fact that a 'satisfactory' interim dividend issued by Courtaulds at this time had helped to calm market fears in this area.

Five days after his disappearance, the state of the markets was calm enough for the *Daily Herald* to make a summary under the column for City Affairs on 9 July that had as its headline: 'No Cause for Scare'.

It said that the loss of Loewenstein was as unlikely to have an effect on the investment markets as the death of James White. It described both men as 'manipulators of the markets' but neither had created anything endurable, as it was put. White was English and had far overreached himself, leaving himself hundreds of thousands of pounds short of being able to meet his commitments.

Although not directly related to his business dealings, amongst the turmoil created by Loewenstein's death, during the following month, the press reported that five puppies were made the subject of an order by the Ministry of Agriculture and Fisheries to be placed in quarantine. They were described as belonging to the executors of Captain Loewenstein.

The whole issue of opening the main door of the plane to the outside was central to what followed in the analysis of what had happened to Loewenstein. Once his body was found, two things could be assumed: that Loewenstein had fallen from the door of the aircraft and the body was indeed that of Loewenstein and not somebody else. All the theories and suppositions that were to follow, quite literally, hinged on the door itself.

He was 51 years old at the time of his death; he did not smoke or drink and rode horses regularly, and he was in reasonably good health but did not possess great strength. The charge that Loewenstein had maybe tried to open the wrong door because he had had one too many drinks cannot be levelled in this case because he was teetotal.

The main door of the Fokker VII was a very basic wooden affair. As can be seen in pictures of the aircraft, the door was reasonably wide at 4ft and it was 6ft in height. It was made of two sheets of plywood on a wooden frame and was attached to the forward part of the fuselage with two hinges. What kept the door and fuselage together was two drop-down bolts through the hinges. The locking mechanism was also fairly basic and consisted of a spring-controlled latch with a handle on the inside of the aircraft. There were also two small interior bolts that were attached before take-off. As far as health and safety standards went, it was typical of its time and did the job for which it was designed.

The reporting of the French judicial inquiry in the newspapers also carried a piece stating that 'well known airmen' at Le Bourget Airport had stated to the press that it would be extremely difficult to open the door of a plane while it was flying. This view contrasted sharply with the statement already made by Donald Drew that it would be possible for Loewenstein to have opened the door during the flight and that he, Drew, had done so himself.

The magistrate investigating the case made a statement that was published on 11 July that Drew stated that he and the mechanic (Robert Little) had been able to open the door of the Fokker VII on its return flight to Croydon. He (the magistrate) finished by saying that the Belgian authorities had no jurisdiction in the case as the plane was registered in Britain and Loewenstein had fallen into English or French waters.

For a man who, according to the aviation press, usually had little to say for himself, Drew seemed to have plenty to say about the door to anyone who would listen. He was known to be a talker and raconteur in private company but said little in more formal situations. That he had so much to say about the door seemed odd, particularly as he contradicted himself. And not only that; others who carried out their own tests contradicted the conclusions that Drew had officially stated. In an interview with the *Evening Standard*, Drew said that he did not consider Loewenstein had committed suicide and that the act of him falling had just happened in some way. He also said in the same interview that he could not be certain if Loewenstein would have been heavy enough to fall out of the door. However, shortly after this statement to the newspaper, Drew and the mechanic, Robert Little, were required to attend the hearing in Brussels on 9 July that had been organised by Madeleine Loewenstein. As already stated, the purpose of this hearing was to get a death certificate issued as quickly as possible and at the hearing Drew stated both he and Little had conducted their own experiments in flight and found that the door could be opened easily against the slipstream. It was a direct contradiction of what he had said to the *Evening Standard* only a few days earlier and it is surprising he was not picked up on it. Could it have been that Drew may have realised that what he had said to the newspaper raised awkward questions about what had really happened? If it was almost impossible to open the door in flight, then how did Loewenstein fall out unless he was forced? Another reason that Drew may have contradicted himself was that he would have been aware Madeleine Loewenstein wanted the death certificate issued as quickly as possible and by changing his story to say that it was relatively easy to fall out of the door then it could be concluded that Loewenstein had simply opened the wrong door and fallen to his death. To suggest otherwise would be to open up the possibility of foul play, which an examining magistrate would certainly look at under those circumstances. As it was, the Belgian magistrate was not happy about what he had heard and refused to grant a death certificate. He was critical of the French authorities for not fully investigating the death.

The story of the door did not end there, however. On 12 July, three days after the magistrates hearing in Brussels, Drew and Little took off from Croydon Airport in the same Fokker, G-EBYI, to conduct further experiments on the door. They were accompanied by Major J.F.C. Cooper, who was the Inspector of Accidents for the Air Ministry, and Jimmy Jeffs. Jeffs was described as an Air Ministry observer, but he actually worked in the Croydon control tower and was well known in aviation circles. Cooper wanted to check the story out for himself and conduct his own experiment. Based on how things went, Cooper was then going to consider whether any modifications would be necessary to the door to make it safer and liaise with the manufacturers accordingly. Once the Fokker had gained 4,000ft (1,219m) altitude, Cooper ran at the door and barged it with his shoulder. The door edged open 6in (15cm) before the slipstream and wash from the propeller forced it shut again. With Drew actually flying the aircraft, Cooper then tied himself to mechanic Robert Little and Jimmy Jeffs. Once he was sure that he was secure and with both Little and Jeffs ready to haul him back when required, Cooper then launched himself at the door again. This time Cooper was able to get the door open just far enough to get his foot outside and onto the step just below, but no more. The force of the slipstream on the wide surface area of the door was tremendous. After the Fokker landed, Cooper's conclusion was that no safety modifications to the door were necessary. What this conclusion meant, without saying it, was that Loewenstein's death could not have been an accident, although it would be a further week before his body would be found floating in the Channel.

All the reports in the newspapers state that after the discovery that Loewenstein was no longer in the aircraft, Drew had immediately circled the sea to look for him before landing 'on the coast' to report the matter to the police. The aviation magazine *Flight* gave a report in its issue dated 12 July (which was eight days after he had fallen from the Fokker) confirming that Drew had gone back to search for Loewenstein. The same *Flight* report also stated that tests had been made with machines since the accident to prove the likelihood of a man being able to open a cabin door in flight and it had been proved to be very difficult to do. The report conceded that it had been said it was possible to open the door in flight. What the report did not say was what these machines were or whether it referred to other aircraft and when the tests were carried out, particularly as it had only been a week since the accident to publication of the report.

Drew's odd statements about the ease of opening the aircraft door in flight was not the only time he made contradictory statements. Sometime after landing at Croydon after flying the Fokker back from Saint-Inglevert, he was interviewed by a correspondent from the *New York Times*.

This interview was not part of any formal enquiries by the authorities, but despite being known for his supposed reticence, Drew openly spoke to the correspondent about what had happened when it was discovered the businessman had fallen from the plane. Drew said that on hearing the news, his first impulse was to turn the aircraft around and head back and descend to start searching for Loewenstein. However, he said, he immediately thought better of it as it was obvious that Loewenstein would have died immediately upon hitting the water from 4,000ft (1,219m). What he was saying was certainly true, but he gave another interview that same day to *The Times* newspaper in which he implied that immediately he had heard the news of Loewenstein's disappearance he had turned back to search as he said nothing could be seen. It was an ambiguous statement and possibly Drew had intended it to be so to show himself as a dutiful employee who had done everything he could to help his employer.

Probably the most contentious theory is that Loewenstein was murdered. It may seem an outlandish idea, but it was nevertheless a distinct possibility. The flight from Croydon to Haren, Brussels, was scheduled to take approximately two hours, so a relatively short flight. Had there been an intention to murder Loewenstein, it would have made it easier to overpower him in the area next to the toilet and where the main door opened out. However, on such a short flight, there was no guarantee that he would have felt the need to answer the call of nature. As it was, and considering he was supposedly engrossed with reading, it would have required overpowering him in his seat in the middle of the cabin.

Loewenstein's seat was facing forward and it was forward of the two seats where the two stenographers sat. To manoeuvre him around these seats while he would be struggling would have been very difficult. All the while there would be the great distress such a scene would be causing to everyone there, including the two young stenographers.

The main point though is that if he was murdered by being overpowered or incapacitated and thrown out of the plane at 4,000ft (1,219m), then every single person on board the aircraft must have either been in on it, or if they weren't then they must have seen what happened and were either bribed or threatened into silence. If Loewenstein had gone into the toilet, it can be assumed that the action of overpowering him took place when he came out into the small area by the door. What would have made it easier to throw him out of the door would have been to overpower and tie him up in the cabin and then carry him bodily to the cabin door. However, the ropes would have had to be removed before throwing him out. A struggle would have ensued with Loewenstein probably realising what was being planned for him by the aircraft door. It wouldn't have made any sense.

The possibility that two of the men, say the mechanic, Robert Little and his valet Fred Baxter were waiting for him as he came out of the toilet doesn't make much sense either. For them to have grabbed him as he came out of the toilet would have meant struggling in an area that wasn't much bigger than a phone box space-wise. Whilst Loewenstein was not a young man and not of a powerful build, the fact that he would have realised he was about to be thrown to his death would have made him do every-thing physically possible to try and stop them pushing him through the door. Added to which, the slipstream would have been pressing hard against the door, which would have made the situation extremely difficult for his attackers. Apart from anything else, a violent struggle would likely have left marks and bruising on the body. Despite being 51 years old, he was in good condition for his age and took regular boxing lessons with a trainer, so he could have put up some kind of a fight. Any injuries he sustained in a fight or struggle could have been picked up at an autopsy. Although the attackers may have thought his body might never be found in the sea, there was also a good chance that it could be found fairly quickly as the English Channel was a busy sea lane.

An alternative would have been to subdue him in some way so that he was unaware of what was happening. For instance, if he had been seated, chloroform could have been used to knock him out, or a sedative of some kind put in food or drink he took. It would have been much easier to carry his body to the door of the aircraft and then, while one or more of the men on board pushed the door open against the slipstream, one of the others could have forced his body out in the open gap of the door and fuselage. Even with two men doing this, it would not have been easy. With Drew flying the aircraft, and assuming he was aware of what was going on in the rear, he could have maybe reduced power to the engines to reduce the airflow against the door. The cruising speed of the Fokker VII was 110 knots (equivalent to 126.5mph), so he could not reduce the speed by much or the aircraft would stall.

Journalist William Norris, in his book *The Man Who Fell from the Sky*, favoured the story that Loewenstein was murdered by being pushed or thrown from the door of the aircraft. It had been explained to Norris that it was relatively easy to loosen the hinges on the door by reaching from the rear aircraft window that could be opened by sliding it forward. When Loewenstein was pushed out of the door, it gave way and he fell to his death. The large plywood door would also have fallen to the sea. The matter of a missing door when the Fokker landed on the beach at Fort-Mardyck was explained by a spare door and bolts kept in the rear compartment of the Fokker to replace the door after landing. This theory also goes some way to answering the question as to why Drew landed the aircraft on the beach at Fort-Mardyck and hadn't continued for a few more minutes to land at Saint-Inglevert aerodrome. There was a good chance the door would not be immediately noticed on the beach if the port side of the aircraft was facing the sea, but on landing at Saint-Inglevert it would probably be noticed immediately.

Whilst it all seems plausible, there are a number of problems with this theory. Firstly, why go to all the trouble of attaching another door, especially with the danger of the original one being found? It was made of wood and would have floated. Furthermore, it would not have fallen too far from Loewenstein's body so there was a good chance (and risk) that if the body was found fairly quickly, the possibility was the door would also be found. If this happened, there would be some very awkward questions indeed for the other occupants of the Fokker. It seems a big risk to take, especially for people who were not professional murderers. A safer scenario would have been to loosen the door fittings, throw the hapless financier out of it and then land with the door missing and say he must have fallen against it and that the faulty fitting gave way and he fell to his death.

There would also be another problem with loosening the fittings. In order for the door to give way, the window would have to be slid forward so someone could reach out to start loosening the fittings. Unless Loewenstein had already been overpowered at this point, he would have wondered what was going on and become concerned at the very least, as there would be no possible excuse why anybody should have needed to open a window in flight and start doing something to the hinges of the door. The whole exercise was fraught with difficulty and danger, with too many possibilities for something to go wrong and be caught out. While murder was not at the forefront of anyone's minds after the disappearance, there were many unanswered questions and it would only need one astute investigator to pick up an anomaly and the whole plot would unravel. Anyone who plotted this must have been aware that the penalty for such a cold-blooded murder would be a death sentence or life imprisonment.

One problem with the witness statements concerned the door leading onto the vestibule and toilet area. The door that led from the aircraft main cabin area also acted as the toilet door. It was hinged so that when it was opened to walk into the vestibule area, the passenger would walk into the toilet area to shut the door behind them. This left the door space open so that anyone in the cabin could see directly into the vestibule, as the door, in effect, was open because it was acting as the closed toilet door to the left, looking towards the rear from the cabin. The two stenographers, Paula Bidalon and Eileen Clarke, were both seated in two seats looking towards the rear and at an angle that would enable them to see the main door into the aircraft on the fuselage, i.e. the door that Loewenstein was supposed to have fallen from. If Loewenstein came out of the toilet he would have had to close that same door so it closed off any view from the cabin to prevent anybody seeing what he was doing, assuming he was going to jump. However, the problem with all this is that Loewenstein's valet, Fred Baxter, said in his statement that when he became concerned at the length of time Loewenstein was taking, he went to the rear of the aircraft and knocked on the door. He said nothing about knocking on the door as it led into the vestibule. Had he meant this surely he would have said that he knocked on the door that led into the vestibule area and he checked that and the toilet area to find no sign of his boss. Neither area was large, so a glance would have sufficed, but the implication in his statement is that the door to the toilet was locked with no sign of Loewenstein. It could be that Baxter meant he knocked on the door leading into the vestibule but his statement was not clear.

Whilst it might seem incredible that Loewenstein was thrown to his death and could only have been thrown to his death by members of his own staff, the question has to be asked: did they hate him that much that they all colluded together to get rid of him? The answer has to be no, because he was generally regarded as being very good to his employees and treated them well. As a businessman he may have upset a good number of people in his business dealings, any number of whom who felt that Loewenstein had crossed them could have nursed grudges against him. The very nature of his dealings meant that other businessmen would be cut out of deals or would lose money as a result of Loewenstein's actions and could wish him ill. However, would the loss of money or a business deal or some sharp practice make that person want to gain revenge by killing Loewenstein? It is perfectly possible, but what stretches credulity is that person or persons would have had to have access to Loewenstein's staff and then persuade them to murder him. Assuming only one (or possibly two people) were persuaded to do so, they would have then had to convince the others (five others in total) to go along with the plan. Presumably they would have had to be offered some kind of substantial financial inducement to go along with it.

There could have been many business rivals who were bitter enough to have arranged his murder. One of the more unlikely business ventures attributed to Loewenstein is that he had got together with American gangster Arnold Rothstein and planned to mass import opiates, including heroin, into the United States. At the time heroin could still be legally manufactured in Europe, which presumably was the attraction from Rothstein's point of view. Not long before he died, Loewenstein and Rothstein had reportedly met in a hotel in East

Forty-Second Street, New York, to discuss the venture, which Loewenstein would have viewed as a sale of opiates that were legally available in Europe. While Loewenstein more than likely had one or two sharp business practices under his belt by this stage, Rothstein was a nasty piece of work and had control of the drugs trade on the eastern seaboard of the USA. Through corruption and bribery he had any number of the police and judiciary in his pocket. It was supposedly the biggest drug deal in the world at the time. Although it was not said directly, there is an implication that Loewenstein had either got on the wrong side of Rothstein or crossed him in some way, which had led to the financier's death. Rothstein had a propensity for violence and his way of dealing with people who gave him problems was to simply have them murdered.

Another possibility is that his wife, Madeleine, was having an affair with the pilot, Donald Drew. Drew was a known womaniser during his time with Imperial Airways. However, Drew had only been flying for Loewenstein for a few months and would not have had a great deal of contact with Madeleine as she rarely accompanied her husband on his trips. The two did know each other though and this was probably because she had used the aircraft to travel between their properties in Europe. It seems a stretch that in the space of twelve weeks or so Drew would have charmed her and she would then have embroiled him in a plot to murder her husband. Unlikely but not impossible.

Some have pointed to the report in the *Daily Herald* on 9 July 1928 when Madeleine Loewenstein had summoned all the senior staff to her chateau. She had rejected any suggestion that he had faked his own death and disappeared. But the question is: How could she have known for sure on this date because the body had not been found at that point and might never have been found for all she knew?

The whole concept of her arranging her husband's murder appears preposterous and yet, the theory of murder seems a strong possibility to explain how Loewenstein met his end.

The theory that Loewenstein had committed suicide was perhaps the most obvious. The *Daily Herald* report on 9 July referred to statements from everyone on board who reported that Loewenstein was in good spirits and laughed and chatted with them, which did not suggest someone preoccupied with thoughts of suicide.

Various accounts of Loewenstein committing suicide take no note of the fact that he was a devout Catholic. The act of suicide breaks the fifth commandment ('Thou shalt not kill') and is considered a mortal sin. Suicide is viewed as murder of the self and is contrary to the love of God, self, family, friends and neighbours. To the twenty-first century atheist and agnostic observers of Loewenstein's possible suicide, they would most likely regard all the reasoning as superstitious mumbo jumbo. However, for someone like Loewenstein, who was a devout believer, it would be the most monumental decision of his life. Not so much the taking of his own life but what happened afterwards. In his own mind he was about to be judged by God as to whether he was fit to enter the Kingdom of Heaven after committing a mortal sin just beforehand. If he stood before the aircraft door getting ready to push it open and jump, the possibility of his soul being damned for eternity was almost certain and would make the strongest believer pause for thought. The Catholic Church allows for some mitigation in individual cases of suicide. These include such things as grave psychological disturbance, anguish, grave fear of hardship, torture and suffering. Loewenstein had no worries about grave hardship and he wasn't being tortured, but he could have been suffering extreme mental anguish. His behaviour in the aircraft cabin prior to his disappearance did not suggest any kind of inner turmoil according to the witnesses. However, despite these supposedly extenuating circumstances, in the eyes of the Catholic Church it is still not morally permissible to commit suicide. In Loewenstein's case, it was not something he could take a briefing or considered opinion on before he jumped. God would be the only judge and the judgment would take place after his death.

One other factor that argues against the suicide theory is that when Loewenstein arrived at Croydon airport for his flight, he went into the terminal building to make a phone call to Sir Herbert Holt. Holt was a Canadian businessman visiting London and Loewenstein had called to arrange to meet him for dinner the following week, after his return from his trip to Brussels. The call was overheard by Robert McIntosh. McIntosh was a pilot nicknamed 'All Weather McIntosh' who was well known in aviation circles at the time and would later become a senior pilot with aviation group Airwork Ltd. McIntosh confirmed the content of the call Loewenstein made. If

Loewenstein had planned on killing himself by stepping out of the plane in roughly an hour's time from when he made the call, it would seem a pointless exercise to be arranging to meet Holt the following week.

One argument is that possibly Loewenstein was not completely aware of what he was doing because it was a new aircraft and he was not familiar with the layout, hence he opened the outside door without thinking. At the time of his disappearance, Loewenstein's Fokker had only been in his possession for exactly five weeks. It was registered in the UK on Wednesday, 30 May, and he had fallen from the aircraft on Wednesday, 4 July. Whilst there may have been some leeway prior to the legal date of registration, it was a brand-new aircraft and had only been given its Dutch registration of H-NAEK for flight testing at the Nederlandsche Vliegtuigenfabriek (Dutch Aircraft Factory) just one week earlier than being registered in the UK. All in all, the aircraft was only six weeks old and it had been in Loewenstein's possession for part of that time. Although an argument could therefore be made that he was not completely familiar with the layout of the cabin and the various doors, he would not have been able to open the outside door using normal pressure because of the sheer force of wind flow on the other side.

The *Manchester Guardian* of 15 August reported that Loewenstein's two brothers-in-law (Maitre Convert and Lieutenant Missone) had asked the distinguished pathologist Dr Paul of Paris to conduct tests during the autopsy to check for the presence of any toxic poisons. Dr Paul duly carried out the tests and in his report delivered to the Belgian authorities, he stated that: 'The clearly characterised trace of toxic matters has been ascertained in the intestines.'

The newspaper article explained that the problem was whose jurisdiction did the investigation of this potential poisoning fall into – France, Belgium or the United Kingdom? The newspaper concluded that as Loewenstein had boarded the aircraft in Croydon in the United Kingdom, it stood to reason that he must have been poisoned before he got on the plane, so therefore it was a British matter to be investigated. Loewenstein's two brothers-in-law had stated to the press that he had been in good health before he boarded the aircraft and that whilst he was on board he had removed his necktie and collar, which may have pointed to breathing difficulties. The collar and necktie were later found by Madeleine when she travelled to Calais and Saint-Inglevert. The two brothers-in-law also explained to the press that Alfred was not known to be unduly worried about anything and that his business affairs were in good order, so there was no motive for him to even consider suicide. Even if it had been true that Loewenstein had been poisoned and was suffering from its effects after he had boarded the aircraft, it would have made him even less likely to be able to force the door to the outside open if he was feeling weak and unable to breathe properly.

As it turned out the following day, the whole poison story was turned on its head when the *Guardian* updated its story of the previous day to say that it was not now believed that Loewenstein had been poisoned. The article explained that a magistrate in Boulogne had explained there was no need for any alarm over the reports of poison found in Loewenstein's body as he was in the frequent habit of taking purgatives. The article went on to say that Loewenstein frequently took overdoses of purgatives, which would have produced an abnormal amount of toxic matter. The financier had visited the toilet shortly after the aircraft left the English coast and it was on a second subsequent visit that the tragedy occurred.

None of this explains how Loewenstein was able to open the outside door on his own. On the same day as the *Guardian* explained the reason for the presence of the toxic matter, the French newspaper *Le Matin* gave an account of a Professor Kohn-Abrest, director of the Laboratoire de Toxicologia, who had also examined Loewenstein's organs and concluded that there were no traces of toxic matter to justify the statement that Loewenstein had been poisoned. In fact, the professor went further and stated that all he found was the contents of a meal and seawater in the organs.

There were a number of peculiar aspects to the whole story. For instance, at the time that Loewenstein's body was found, a mystery letter was sent by a woman to the French judicial authorities, who passed the letter to the widow's lawyer. The contents of this letter were never revealed, but the French authorities had obviously taken it seriously enough to pass it on to Madeleine Loewenstein's lawyer.

Another peculiarity is the seeming lack of interest by the authorities in England, France and Belgium in getting to the bottom of what actually happened.

The part played by pilot Donald Drew also raised a number of unanswered questions. He was ambiguous as to whether he had turned the aircraft around to look for Loewenstein after he was informed of his disappearance. Many questioned why he chose to land on the beach at Fort-Mardyck instead of continuing to Saint-Inglevert aerodrome, just a few minutes flying time further on. Many have also questioned why he didn't use his radio to inform the aerodrome of what had happened. There was also his conflicting versions of whether the door could be opened easily in flight or not.

When a reporter put the question to an Imperial Airways representative as to why Drew had not returned from Brussels after he went over for the inquiry, the response was that he was remaining there of his own volition. The implication contained in the question was that Drew was not being allowed to return from Brussels by the authorities. There were rumours that the plane had been 'sequestered' by the British Air Ministry and this was reported as fact by one news agency. However, the Imperial Airways representative was keen to dispel the rumour and said that, although they had been asked not to fly it by the Air Ministry, it was in a hangar at Croydon, was not under any kind of guard, and could be accessed by anyone. The fact was, though, that the plane belonged to the Loewenstein estate, not Imperial Airways, as the Imperial representative pointed out.

Another anomaly concerned ownership of the aircraft and Drew. When Madeleine Loewenstein had inspected the Fokker at Saint-Inglevert aerodrome, she told Drew to get rid of it. It was reported that the aircraft had been bought by Glen Kidston, a well-known aviator, explorer and car enthusiast. This may be the case but the official British registration document shows it registered to Donald Drew, C/O Imperial Airways, from the date Loewenstein took delivery of it. It then shows the date of change of ownership as March 1930 (with a question mark beside the actual day). On 29 October 1928, Glen Kidston left Croydon with Drew as pilot in G-EBYI on its way to East Africa for a safari trip and big game hunting. On 15 November 1928, the aircraft had an accident in Mongola in the Sudan. The occupants were unharmed but the aircraft was seriously damaged. The aircraft was recovered and taken back to the factory in Schiphol for extensive repairs. A test flight was made from Schiphol aerodrome on 29 November 1929. What happened to the Fokker (identified by its construction number 5063) thereafter is not known for certain. The Fokker archive appears to show that it may have been sold to the Italian National Electricity Company CONIEL with the registration I-FERO. It was later believed to have been sold in Ethiopia in 1938 and its eventual fate is unknown.

One final item worthy of mention is what Loewenstein was doing before he disappeared. In the period before he got up to go to the toilet at the back of the aircraft, there appear to be two versions of the statements of his staff. One version has Loewenstein talking and joking with his staff and the other has him reading a book. In his obituary in *The Times,* it clearly stated that he never read a book or a newspaper and seldom wrote letters when a telegram would do. In short, he was a man who regarded these activities as eating into precious time, so the obvious question is: can the statements made be true that he was reading a book prior to the moments before his death or had he changed the habit of a lifetime and suddenly taken up reading as a way to relax? It seems unlikely and makes the observations by his staff most peculiar. They were with him much of the time and would have known if he was a regular reader, so why mention it if he wasn't? If the intention was to give the impression that Loewenstein was relaxed before he fell from the aircraft, it is odd they would mention something that he would never normally do (reading a book). On the other hand, if there was a violent altercation where he was overpowered before being thrown from the door, to say he was reading a book beforehand is something of a distraction. Because there was no full police investigation into the death, this discrepancy was not picked up. Perhaps a more pressurised and aggressive police interview of all the staff present might have yielded a different story.

The eventual fates of some of the party of six who were present with Loewenstein are interesting. If he had been murdered, then theoretically the business rivals (or Madeleine Loewenstein) who had wanted Loewenstein 'done away with' would show half a dozen people who had mysteriously come into some wealth as their pay-offs. Yet this did not appear to be the case, although nothing is known about what became of Paula Bidalon, the French-born stenographer, or the other stenographer, Eileen Clarke. Donald Drew was to die of cancer and Arthur Hodgson and Robert Little appeared to have led uneventful lives until they passed away. However, the eventual fate of Fred Baxter, Loewenstein's valet, made many observers of this tragedy take notice. Baxter had carried on working for Loewenstein's son, Robert, in the same position

Loewenstein

Loewenstein's Fokker VII just prior to delivery to him, seen here with its Dutch registration H-NAEK used for flight testing at the Nederlandsche Vliegtuigenfabriek (Dutch Aircraft Factory). (*Martin Smit, Aviodrome Collection, Lelystad*)

Philadelphia Airport, 5 May 1928 – Alfred Loewenstein (centre) after having just walked through the Fokker's propellers, narrowly escaping serious injury. Left, Mrs Philip Boyer; Right, E.T. Stotesbury of Drexel & Co. The door is the same as the one that would figure in Loewenstein's death two months later. (*Shutterstock*)

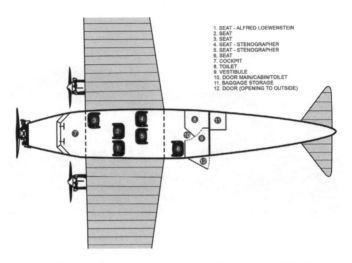

1. SEAT - ALFRED LOEWENSTEIN
2. SEAT
3. SEAT
4. SEAT - STENOGRAPHER
5. SEAT - STENOGRAPHER
6. SEAT
7. COCKPIT
8. TOILET
9. VESTIBULE
10. DOOR MAIN/CABIN/TOILET
11. BAGGAGE STORAGE
12. DOOR (OPENING TO OUTSIDE)

Drawing of Loewenstein's Fokker VII interior. (*bhardwaz – FIVERR*)

The interior of a normal Fokker VII configured for ordinary airline passenger operations. (*Martin Smit, Aviodrome Collection, Lelystad*)

The Dover tug *Lady Brassey* was chartered by pilot Donald Drew and mechanic Robert Little to search in the English Channel for Loewenstein's body. (*Copyright Alex Duncan via Nigel Thornton*)

he had held with his father. On 22 April 1932, Baxter shot himself in Robert Loewenstein's apartment in Paris, using Robert's revolver. Baxter had supposedly killed himself after Robert had gone out for two hours, leaving him on his own. One of the reasons given was that Baxter had borrowed money from Robert, which he had spent on gambling and drinking, and could not pay it back, although this is disputed. It was felt that Baxter knew exactly what had happened to Robert's father (i.e. that he had been murdered) and was unable to keep it in any longer, so he told Robert. As to whether Robert shot Baxter in a fit of rage or Robert, on hearing the dreadful truth went out for two hours, only to come back and find Baxter dead, is debatable. Either way, the whole case looked somewhat suspicious considering the background.

Robert Loewenstein was to meet his own death through aviation. During the Second World War he had joined the Air Transport Auxiliary (ATA), whose purpose was to deliver aircraft to their units around the country. On 29 March 1941 he was flying Bristol Blenheim IV serial V6263 from Liverpool's Speke aerodrome to RAF Lyneham when an engine cut out and he crashed a mile south-west of White Waltham. He was initially buried in St Andrew Churchyard in Twyford but his remains were later repatriated to Belgium.

Less than two years after Loewenstein's death, a Hollywood film (named *Such Men are Dangerous*) was made that was loosely based on his life. During the filming of an air sequence in January 1930, two Stinson Detroiter aircraft of Tanner Air Tours acted as camera aircraft and were filming an air sequence involving the re-enactment of Loewenstein's fall using a Lockheed Vega. The two Stinson aircraft collided and crashed. Everyone in both aircraft (a total of ten people) was killed, including Kenneth Hawks, the brother of well-known director Howard Hawks.

There are no easy answers among the theories to explain what actually happened to Alfred Loewenstein. Although he was buried in an unmarked and nondescript grave and despite the fact his body had decomposed considerably when it was first found, there seems to be no dispute that it was him. In other words, he had not quietly arranged to disappear for the rest of his life and leave a substitute body in his place. His devout Catholicism and its strictures regarding suicide argue against the suicide theory, quite apart from the fact it appears it would have been impossible to push the door open on his own. Incredible though it may seem, the murder theory is the one that stands out as being plausible. It is a murder theory in which some theorists have his wife, Madeleine, as the instigator with all six of his staff on board the flight being complicit and staying silent for the rest of their lives. It is notable that Madeleine did not attend her husband's funeral. If this is all true and she had been involved to control the wealth, she did not enjoy it for long as she died in 1938, only ten years later, in Paris.

ACKNOWLEDGEMENTS AND SOURCES

I would like to thank Amy Rigg at The History Press for her advice and encouragement; Kathleen Huggett, Anthony Middleton and Triona McCloskey for their kind help with proofreading and helping out with the last-minute panic (my panic) of putting a book together.

Chapter 1 – The Isle of Mull Cessna

I feel a personal affinity to this story because, as a young lad, I used to plane spot at Edinburgh's Turnhouse Airport in the late 1960s and early '70s. It was a much quieter airport then with not a great deal of activity. G-AVTN was then part of the 'Jock' Dalgleish stable of Cessnas. I often used to watch it taxi from its parking spot by the Edinburgh Flying Club, out to take-off and land on runway 08/26, as it was in those days.

I would like to thank the following (in no particular order): Dr Felicity Grainger, who kindly spared me the time to describe what must still be a painful memory; members and former members of Glasgow Flying Club; Dougie Martindale for the kind permission to use his late father's (John Martindale) excellent photo of G-AVTN at Turnhouse. John was one of the stalwarts of the Glasgow aviation scene from that time.

I am also very grateful to Calum Finnigan for a lot of footwork and the photo of the Sound of Mull looking over to the Glenforsa strip from Lochaline. If you are into diving, I can recommend his business at Eat Sleep Dive Lochaline Ltd, Lochaline Dive Centre, O2 cafe and bunkhouse, Lochaline, Morvern, Argyll, PA80 5XT.

I want to make a special mention of Richard Grieve for very kindly sending me the slides he took in September 1986 of the wreckage of what I am certain is G-AVTN and for his account of what he saw that day.

I would like to also quickly mention Michael Hurwitz, the archivist for the London Philharmonia Orchestra, for giving me background and also for sharing his father's memories of Peter Gibbs during his time with the orchestra.

Tom Wright at the London Philharmonic Orchestra for answering my queries.

Files:
National Register of Scotland File No. SC57/12A/1976/1
National Archive File Air 27/426/1 41 Squadron ORB
National Archive File Air 27/426/28 41 Squadron ORB

Books:
Blood, Sweat and Valour – 41 Squadron RAF, August 1942–May 1945: A Biographical History by Steve Brew (Fonthill Media, 2012, ISBN 978-1-7815-5193-6)
Sing Low My Sweet Chariot: Memories of a Musical Foot Soldier, 1947–1987 by John Honeyman (Plastic Comb, 1998, No ISBN)

Further interesting detail can be found on wrecks in the area around the Isle of Mull and Oban from SAMPHIRE (Scottish Atlantic Maritime Past: Heritage, Investigation, Research & Education)

Magazines:
Flight Global Archives: www.flightglobal.com

Quotes and Comments:
The comments regarding the behaviour of Peter Gibbs at the Glasglow Flying Club were made to me in February 2017.

The quote 'A strange man' was made by Michael Hurwitz's father, who played in the London Philharmonia Orchestra.

Quotes made in the FAI are taken from the testimony (Source: National Register of *Scotland File No. SC57/12A/1976/1).*

Chapter 2 – The Kennedy Curse

I would like to thank Maryrose Grossman and Arabella Matthews at the John F. Kennedy Presidential Library and Museum, Boston, Massachusetts,

I am also very grateful to Dr Douglas A. Lonnstrom, Professor of Statistics at Siena College. Dr Lonnstrom holds a flying licence and has more than twenty years' experience flying. He has studied the accident for ten years and had flown in the same area on the day of the accident. For those who would like to delve deeper into the background of the accident, I recommend Dr Lonnstrom's excellent book *JFK Jr: 10 Years After the Crash, A Pilot's Perspective* published by Northeast Tee Time LLC, 2009, ISBN 978-0-9668-4722-2.

Second-hand copies can be obtained from Amazon or you can order a signed copy directly from him at Siena College, 515 Loudon Rd, Loudonville, NY 12211, USA.

Files:
NTSB Report Identification No. NYC99MA178 (Summary of Accident Report)

Newspapers:
The Guardian (19 July 1999): There are thirteen articles covering aspects of the loss of John F. Kennedy Jr's aricraft, including the address of President Clinton.
www.theguardian.com/us-news/kennedy/1999/jul/19/all
The Globe (15 June 2009): There are nine articles covering aspects of the loss of John F. Kennedy Jr's aircraft.
www.bostonglobe.newspapers.com/search/#query=john+kennedy+jr&ymd=1999-07-19

Magazines and Articles:
'JFK Jr – 10 Years After' by Barry Chamish, published 4 September 2009: www.samsonblinded.org/news/jfk-jr-ten-years-after-13855
Professional Pilot Rumour Neteo: www.pprune.org
'Why was Rabin Murdered', www.vaam.tripod.com/Jun2498.html

The statement issued by the White House (under President William J Clinton) during the search operation (p.79/80): www.govinfo.gov/content/pkg/CDOC-106sdoc7/html/CDOC-106sdoc7.html

TWA 800 accident details: www.aviation-safety.net – TWA 800.

Chapter 3 – Kinross Incident

I would like to thank the following people for their contributions: USAF Report of Aircraft Accident 23 November 1953 (Dept of the Air Force, HQ Air Force Safety Agency); Lt Col Louis J. Nigro, MI ANG (Ret) Executive Director at the Selfridge Military Air Museum; Dr Layne Karafantis (formerly of the Smithsonian Institution); and Randall Smith.

I would also like to particularly thank the following:

Former F-89 Scorpion crew member USAF Brigadier General (*ret.*) Mike DiBernardo who described to me the characteristics of the F-89 and sitting on alert status.

Former F-89 Scorpion USAF pilot (*ret.*) Tom McCarthy, who flew both the D and J Model F-89s and told me how they handled and what it was like to sit on alert status. Tom said that practice interceptions were made regularly with US-bound airliners along with the occasional 'real thing' – Soviet Tu-95 'Bear' bombers. Also, all homeward-bound SAC overseas deployments were routinely intercepted. His view is that the F-89 is sometimes unfairly criticised and pointed out that the USAF Northeast Air Command rocket team won the 1956 William Tell Rocket meet with the type, using tactics that called for higher airspeeds and was highly successful. For those interested, Tom has flown (in addition to the F-89D and F-89J) the F-100, F-102, F-106 and the F-15, with the F-106 coming out as his favourite.

The Mutual UFO Network Inc (MUFON) for permission to describe their excellent research into the Great Lakes Dive Company.

Dave Pengilly, UFO★BC director, and Gord Heath for their kind permission to quote from their research.

For his kind help, I would like to extend my thanks to Brett Stolle, NH-03 Manuscript Curator, National Museum of the US Air Force Research Division/MUA, Wright Patterson AFB, Ohio.

I would also like to thank RCAF historian Larry Milberry for background information and providing me with the superb photo of the actual RCAF C-47 serial VC-912 that was said to be the subject of the F-89C Scorpion's interception.

I am also grateful to Lt General (*Ret.*) David Huddleston CMM, MSC, CD, the former head (Commander, Air Command) of the RCAF, for his help.

I had been provided with contact details for Gerry Fosberg, the Commander of the RCAF C-47 VC-912 that night, but I did not receive any response to my queries.

Interviews:
Mike Wallace Interview – Harry Ransom Center, University of Texas at Austin.

Chapter 4 – Sri Lankan Mystery

I am extremely grateful to Melissa Gottwald at the Aviation Safety & Security Archives, Embry-Riddle Aero -nautical University and Amy Reytar of The National Archives at College Park, MD for pointing me in the right direction with regard to the investigation report into the disappearance.

For a deep analysis of the complexity of Wijewardene's companies, see *Overseas Corporate Structures, which Hide Real Owners: Foreign Business Empire of a Sri Lankan Entrepeneur* by Nihal Sri Ameresekere, ISBN 978-1-4772-1508-1, published by Authorhouse, UK. The ways the companies were set up and their interlinked dealings outside Sri Lanka are examined with suggestions of possible corruption. It is an impressive piece of work.

It has proved difficult to obtain a photo of Learjet 35A N482U. There had been a photo with the original police investigation report but this is now not available. None of the usual aviation photography websites had one and following a request to Bombardier Gates Learjet, which manufactures the jet now, the company informed me that it was not policy to release photos of aircraft that had been produced.

Reports:
Police Report 17 March 1983 signed off by Director, Criminal Investigation Dept., MDA Rajapaksa.

Magazines:
Professional Pilot Rumour Network: www.pprune.org

Aviation Safety: www.aviation–safety.net
Flight Global Archives: www.flightglobal.com

Chapter 5 – Murder, Accident or Suicide?

I would to thank Kathryn Bubien.

I am most grateful to Martin Smit, curator at the Aviodrome Museum and Collection, Lelystad, for his kind help.

The source of the story of gangster Arnold Rothstein and Loewenstein signing up to a deal to import heroin into the USA is Arnold Rothstein's biographer, David Pietrusza. The story is mentioned in the book *Chasing the Scream: The First and Last Days of the War on Drugs* by Johann Hari, published by Bloomsbury in 2015, ISBN 978-1-6204-0890-2.

The registration document for G-EBYI can be seen at www.caa.co.uk/Aircraft-register/G-INFO.

N.B. The Fokker VII has been described in some articles and a book as an 'A' model but the G-INFO registration website has it down as a 'B' model. The scan of the original registration document merely states 'Fokker V.II 8-Seater Monoplane'.

Newspaper archives are accessible online from provincial libraries in the UK, but the Newspaper Reading Room at the British Library in St Pancras, London, is better geared up from a research point of view. The *Daily Express*, *Daily Herald*, *Daily Telegraph* and *The Times* are all on microfilm. The *Illustrated London News*, *Manchester Guardian* and the *New York Times* can be viewed using a British Library PC. Actual print copies of the French newspaper *Le Matin* are held there covering from 1919 to 1944. The article

'Loewenstein's Puppies' is only mentioned in the *Daily Herald*, 11 August 1928

Newspapers:
Daily Express
Daily Herald
Daily Telegraph
The Times
Illustrated London News
Manchester Guardian
Le Matin
New York Times

Books:
The Man Who Fell from the Sky by William Norris (Viking Penguin Inc., 1987, ISBN 978-0-6708-1369-8)

Magazines:
Flight Global Archives: www.flightglobal.com
Aeroplane Magazine November 2007

INDEX

You might also be interested in:

DAVID GERO

AVIATION

DISASTERS

THE WORLD'S MAJOR CIVIL
AIRLINER CRASHES SINCE 1950

SIXTH EDITION

9780750966337